Birds

Chatto Nature Guides

British and European
Birds

Illustrated with colour photographs

Dr Walther Thiede

Translated by Annette Brandeis

Chatto & Windus · London

Published by
Chatto & Windus Ltd.
40 William IV Street
London WC2N 4DF

＊

Clarke, Irwin & Co Ltd
Toronto

British Library Cataloguing in Publication Data
  Thiede, Walther
    British and European birds. —
      (Chatto nature guides).
    1. Birds—Europe—identification
    I. Title II. Thiede, Walther
    598.2'94   QL690
  ISBN 0 7011 2321 4 Hardback
  ISBN 0 7011 2322 2 Paperback

© BLV Verlagsgesellschaft – mbH,
München, 1977
English Translation © Chatto & Windus
Ltd. 1978.

Printed in Italy

Preface

This book is not intended as a complete *Field Guide* (there are many good ones about, although in almost every case the birds are depicted in somewhat lifeless drawings and paintings), but as an introduction to European birds for the beginner bird watcher. In a work of this size it is clearly impossible to depict all of even the most commonly seen species in Britain and continental Europe. What we have done is to illustrate many of them with superb colour photographs showing them in their natural habitat, and to refer in the accompanying text to further like and allied species. Some birds are included which are not seen easily in Britain, but which certainly can be seen by the visitor to continental Europe, such as the White Stork or the Black Kite. Indeed at least two of the woodpeckers depicted are rare vagrants in Britain, but again can be seen in the wooded regions of Europe.

Pictures and text are intended to complement each other. Apart from a description of the bird's most important characteristics, reference is made where necessary to the more frequent species with which it may be confused. Information on each bird's habitat, distribution (including its status as a resident or migrant bird), feeding and breeding habits, and the biological facts which determine the bird's life is given in a succinct and precise form.
We hope these photographs showing birds in their characteristic surroundings may help and encourage identification, whereas sometimes a more formal system may alarm and confuse the amateur.

About Bird Watching

The constant pleasure we get from the songs of birds and their lively behaviour has made many people want to know more about them and to be able to identify them. Many aids are now available to help them to achieve this: reference books, binoculars, records of bird songs, excursions organised by societies, and even package tours to many countries under expert leadership. But all these luxuries are not really necessary, and it might be useful to look at what is essential for observing birds.

Apart from an identification book, which is indispensable, we need a trained eye and ear, patience and a note book. Even now there are among us many seasoned bird watchers who require no other equipment.

The Trained Senses: We must use our senses of both sight and sound when studying birds. In winter we *see* the activity on the bird table; in spring we *hear* the blackbird's song. The more we use and exercise our senses, the more quickly we will succeed in identifying birds not only in isolation (through field glasses), but also by their habits and behaviour in their natural environment. It is not at all easy, for instance, to predict the line of flight or to train one's field glasses on the exact spot where the bird will alight, and the naked eye has to practise this skill.

We must learn to differentiate between the important and the unimportant. The following are important points:
— the field marks described under "Characteristics" and visible in the colour photos
— the shape of the bird
— its typical stance and gait
— its size in relation to specific features of its environment
— its characteristic regular call-notes and song patterns
— its natural environment (habitat)

Patience: There are several good reasons for the need for patience. The most important is undoubtedly that fidgeting and impatience are transmitted to the bird. Mostly it flies away; at best it takes cover or stops in its tracks and gives alarm signals, and so we lose the opportunity of studying the bird's natural behaviour. We realise again and again with surprise and pleasure how much can be observed by simply sitting quietly somewhere in the open and watching, for instance, a pair of tits feeding in the garden, a blackbird brood in a hedge or ducklings with their mother on a town pond.

The Note Book: No observation is too insignificant to be jotted down. Those who follow this golden rule will profit many years later from their diary notes. You should also write down:
— what was expected but *not* seen (unfortunately only very few people do this)
— the habitat in which the bird was observed.
— the time at which it was observed.
You should never postpone writing up your notes till you get home. Few people are able much later to recall all that has been observed.

The Identification Book. Have the book in front of you and look for the bird you are watching or have just seen. Without haste (haste disturbs not only you but also the bird), having memorised gait, size and a few striking characteristics, scan the pictures and find one which largely corresponds to your sighting. Now pause and read the text on the opposite page. Start right away with the section "Characteristics". Glance back at the bird and then tick off the characteristics one by one.
Even if they coincide, you should take the precaution of reading the section "May be confused with". In this way you will avoid coming to wrong conclusions and you will also sharpen your judgment and discrimination. You should then start making notes.

The correct use of the identification book requires practice, but you will soon become familiar with it.

By the way, to try to manage without the identification book once you are more advanced and know the birds is misguided ambition. To do that one must be totally familiar with the species.

I have been bird watching for about 30 years and I still use such an identification book (and I usually carry in my rucksack at least one more guide). Moreover, reading about one thing often acts as a stimulant to further observation, and poses questions which lead to investigations of one's own.

Those who want to make a more thorough study of the world of birds will read the standard reference books, join ornithological societies (in which professional and amateur ornithologists cooperate), and subscribe to an ornithological journal.

The following list may be helpful:

Books:

A Field Guide to the Birds of Britain and Europe; *Peterson, Mountfort and Hollom* (Collins)

The Hamlyn Guide to Birds of Britain and Europe; *Bruun and Singer* (Hamlyn)

Birds of Britain and Europe with N. Africa and Middle East; *Heinzel, Fitter and Parslow* (Collins)

The Popular Handbook of British Birds; *Hollom* (H.F. & G. Witherby)

There are all *identification* guides. For information on where to go to see interesting birds you should consult:

A Guide to Bird Watching in Europe; *Ferguson-Lees, Hockliffe and Zweeres* (Bodley Head)

Where to Watch Birds; *Gooders* (Deutsch)

Societies and Journals:

Royal Society for the Protection of Birds, The Lodge, Sandy, Bedfordshire SG19 2DL; publishes *Birds* six times a year, a highly illustrated magazine, packed with interesting news, facts, and the latest information on the societies reserves; and runs Young Ornithologists Club, with its own publication *Bird Life.*

The British Trust for Ornithology, Beech Grove, Tring, Hertfordshire HP23 5NR; runs many projects and coordinates amateur research. Publishes *Bird Study.*

British Birds; a monthly journal for serious amateurs.

Field Glasses: Most people use field glasses too frequently, but like many technical aids they can both heighten our pleasure and broaden our opportunities for observation. They are invaluable, for instance, for a precise study of plumage, for observation in twilight conditions, at great distances in a difficult environment, and in distant flight observation. In cases of doubt field glasses can help in establishing the crucial point—for example, whether a gull's legs are flesh colour, yellow or greenish-blue.

Moreover, as good prismatic field glasses are cheaper today than ever before, there is no longer any reason for not having them.

In 30 years I have used three pairs: the first was a good solid Zeiss glass 8×30 bought in the thirties; the second a Japanese 7×50 and the present one a Japanese 7×35 glass. I gave away the 7×50 pair as it was so big and too heavy. My personal recommendation is a Japanese Nikon glass 7×35. For eight years now I have been lugging it through all the climatic regions and hazards of Europe and Asia without every having had it repaired. It has merely received a few scratches and dents.

Note:

— The greater the magnification, the smaller the field.

— Try out all glasses outside the shop before making a purchase. Lenses vary and people's eye-sight varies.

— The longer you walk around with your field glasses, the more grateful you are for a light-weight pair.

As far as the bird-watcher is concerned, what matters is not $10 \times$ magnification versus $7 \times$ magnification (which is sufficient), but light intensity, and this is very good in the case of the 7×35.

Bird-Song Records: During any one excursion the novice bird-watcher will recognize the song of only a few species with which he is already acquainted, and will fail to hear the song of others still unknown to him. I have been able to confirm this experience in my own case from many years of foreign travel in unfamiliar terrain. But whenever I had listened beforehand carefully and repeatedly to records of song-birds I expected to hear, I recognised their voices at once. I think it is a good idea, therefore, to buy the standard records of our song-birds.

Excursions Organised by Societies: Excursions of this kind are warmly recommended. The beginner is forced to subject his skills to critical self-examination. With the help of experienced bird watchers he will quickly get to know a number of sounds, songs and movements particular to our birds. With every successful excursion he will take a good step forward.

The satisfaction of achievement and the opportunities for contact with other enthusiastic beginners and helpful experts cannot be overestimated.

Conservation: The reader should be aware of the need for protection and conservation. As man encroaches on the wetlands and on wild country for industry, oil refineries and housing, and as he pollutes rivers and estuaries, so the feeding grounds of many birds are taken over, and the species either retreats or diminishes in numbers. Pesticides on arable land build up in small mammals and so birds of prey lay infertile eggs and the populations decrease. Twenty-five years ago the Barn Owl was a fairly common bird to see round farm buildings; now it is not.

Many birds have decreased as a result of man's greed for land, and the amateur bird watcher should be aware of this. He should also be aware of the great strides made in Britain by many societies, but pre-eminently by the Royal Society for the Protection of Birds, to conserve areas of special attraction for both rare and common birds. They have helped greatly also in pressing for realistic laws to fine egg stealers and having many species placed on a protected list. There are similar movements in other European countries, notably in Holland, Scandinavia and Germany; but there are still great problems in countries such as France and particularly Italy, where millions of birds are annually slaughtered indiscriminately, shot by so-called "hunters".

Any amateur bird watcher seriously interested in helping to conserve our birds and their habitats should join the Royal Society for the Protection of Birds (see under Societies).

Text Explanations

Status: The following status symbols (explanations given below) are intended to be a general guide to the birdwatcher, so that he will know if it is likely the bird he thinks he sees can be present in that locality at that particular time of year. We have not used the commonly employed R for resident, M for migrant etc., for many so-called resident birds migrate to a greater or lesser extent, and the study of migration is another more specialised field outside the scope of this pocket guide.

PB.   Present throughout the year in at least parts of Europe, including at least parts of the British Isles.

PC.   Present throughout the year in at least parts of continental Europe, but not including the British Isles.

SVB.   Summer visitor to parts of Europe, including parts of the British Isles.

SVC.   Summer visitor to parts of Europe, but very rarely to the British Isles.

WVB.   Winter visitor to parts of Europe, including parts of the British Isles.

WVC.   Winter visitor to parts of Europe, but very rarely to the British Isles.

Nesting: No mention is made in the text if one brood per year is usual. These species only breed a second time if they lose their clutch.

Errata

The following errors in the text should be noted:

p. 14 **Mute Swan,** line 7, should read
". . . flesh-coloured . . ."

p. 28 **Buzzard,** line 13 should read ". . . dark broad band;"

p. 52 **Woodpeckers,** line 4, should read "their stiff tail . . ."

p. 100 **Fieldfare,** line 9, page reference should be 98.

p. 102 **Crested Tit,** line 3, should read
". . .May not easily be confused . . ."

p. 142 **Index of English Names**
—the following entries
should be added:

Golden Oriole	132
Starling	130
Whinchat	90

—the following should be
deleted:

Pirol	132

—the following should be
corrected:

Fieldfare	100
Firecrest	84
Willow Warbler	82

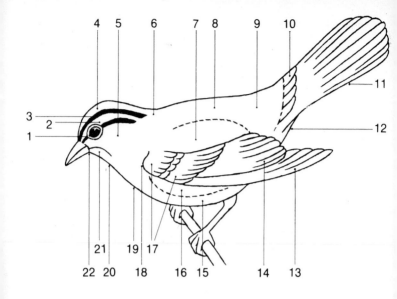

Topography of the Bird

1 Eye-stripe	15 Belly
2 Supercilium	16 Flanks
3 Head-stripe	17 Wing-coverts
4 Crown-stripe	18 Bend of wing
5 Ear-coverts (cheek)	19 Breast
6 Nape	20 Throat
7 Scapulars	21 Moustachial stripe
8 Back	22 Chin
9 Rump	
10 Upper tail-coverts	
11 Outer tail-feathers	
12 Under tail-coverts	
13 Primaries	
14 Secondaries	

The Great Crested Grebe

Podiceps cristatus

The Great Crested Grebe is the most frequently seen of the five grebes living in Europe. They all live on water and are excellently adapted, with their torpedo-shaped bodies, legs projecting from behind used as oars, pointed bills and extremely short tail, to their life of under-water hunting. They are freshwater inhabitants.—**Characteristics:** In its nuptial plumage the Great Crested Grebe is easily recognisable by its rufous-black ruff; in its grey-white winter plumage, its pink bill and white supercilium distinguish it from the Red-Necked Grebe, Podiceps grisegena (only in parts of Britain in winter).—**Habitat:** On largish non-flowing waters; when in passage and in the winter also along the coast and on running water.—**Food:** Mainly fish, water insects, crayfish and tadpoles.—**PB.**—**Nesting:** Near the water's edge, preferably in reed-mace (typha); the floating nest usually contains four eggs; incubation period is 25-29 days; the fledglings are cared for by the parent birds with shared responsibility for 10-11 weeks. Notable for carrying its young, when small, on its back.

Mute Swan

Cygnus olor

Characteristics: The three European swans, the Mute, the Whooper and the Bewick, are white. The bills are red (Mute Swan) or yellow. In the case of the adult Mute Swan it is a brilliant orange red, with a black base, tip and knob. The male has a particularly developed knob. Like other cygnets young Mute Swans have a greyish-brown, dirty-white plumage and pale fresh-coloured bills without knobs; their bills change to yellow-red in their second year. However, the black base of the bill is a distinctive mark. In flight the wings make a loud singing noise.—**Habitat:** Inland waters, to which it is frequently introduced by man. On coasts it appears as a winter visitor and does not breed.—**PB.**—**Food:** Under-water plants easily reached with its long neck, and grass. To help its digestion it eats small stones and earth and presents no threat to fish.—**Nesting:** It builds its large impressive nest on dry soil near the water and lays 5-8 eggs; the incubation period lasts 35-38 days. The cygnets are accompanied for many months by the adult birds.

Heron

Ardea cinerea

A large aquatic bird, frequently seen standing motionless by water. Often sighted thus from a passing train. Known for its communal nesting in heronries. Decreasing, like the Stork, due to reclamation of land and interference with its breeding sites. A generally timid bird.—**Characteristics:** A large light-grey and white bird with black markings, a long neck, which is arched in flight into an S-shape, and a pale yellow dagger-shaped bill. The juveniles have a blackish horn-coloured bill, a black instead of white crown, and they lack the two black plumes on the neck.—**May be confused with** the smaller Purple Heron, Ardea purpurea (not in Britain) which has a chocolate-brown instead of a white neck and a black instead of a white belly.—**Habitat:** On shallow banks of all waters from the sea coast to ditches along railway embankments. In late autumn it visits fields to hunt mice.—**P.B.**—**Food:** It hunts standing motionless and stalking with endless patience. Its main food is fish, and otherwise any animal that comes its way with which it can cope, such as eels, frogs, snakes, mice and insects. It is not fussy and makes do with anything.—**Nesting:** It nests in colonies, known as heronries, in the tops of high woodland trees, rarely in reeds, except in the Netherlands. Also sometimes near or even in cities. The imposing nests, which are made from small branches, contain 3-5 eggs. The incubation period is 25-28 days. The chicks, rarely more than three, leave the colony finally at the age of 8-9 weeks. Both parents feed their young day and night.

The White Stork

Ciconia ciconia

Popular in legend and fairy tale, the Stork is most characteristically recognised nesting on chimneys in north European villages. It depends on extensive water-meadows for the earthworms with which it initially feeds its young. Very rarely seen in Britain. Pest control, cable networks and vanishing marshland have contributed to a serious decline in the numbers of birds to be seen in Europe now. Noted for spectacular migration occurrences, particularly over the Bosporus.—**Characteristics:** Large black and white bird with orange-red bill and legs. In flight distinguished from Heron by extended neck, not bent. Often migrates at great height. Young storks have black bills which later become brown.—**Habitat:** Bogs, damp meadows and shallow water in open country. Travels to its south and east African winter quarters along two fixed routes, via the Straits of Gibraltar and the Bosporus. Young storks from the same nest situated in a wide mixed area east and west of the dividing line may migrate via either route.—**SVC—Food:** Mice, insects, earthworms; to a lesser extent frogs, crayfish, lizards, snakes, fish and even carrion. When returning from their winter quarters, they rely initially almost entirely on earthworms. Grasshoppers and locusts are the main food in the winter quarters.—**Nesting:** The huge nest is free-standing and placed high on buildings, towers, chimneys and trees. The incubation period for the 3-5 eggs is 33-34 days, and the young stay in the nest for 54-63 days after hatching. One of the parent birds constantly guards the nest, up to their fourth week, after which time one of them can raise the young alone. Man-made platforms for nests are welcomed.

Grey Lag Goose

Anser anser

Geese are highly social animals, and their behaviour has been described and interpreted in a fascinating way by Konrad Lorenz. They are long-lived, the birds nearly 50 years old have been known to breed in captivity. Two races of Grey Lag are found in Europe; the Western European and the Eastern European. They breed in parts of Europe, but are seen here mostly as winter visitors. They are greatly at risk, and their numbers can only be maintained by protecting their breeding and winter quarters. Grey Lags are the ancestors of our domestic geese.—**Characteristics:** Identification of the seven grey-brown species of geese of the anser genus is difficult and can only be done on the basis of the colour of the feet and bills. Light and shade can completely mislead the observer. Greylag geese make a silvery grey impression. The thick bill of the western race is a pure deep yellow with a light flesh-coloured top, and that of the eastern race a strong pink. They have a flat forehead. The juveniles are darker and without the narrow white ring on the base of the bill. Legs and feet pinkish, in juveniles greyish-pink.—**Habitat:** They nest on flat moors with open water and on inland lakes. During migration and in winter they stay on grasslands, arable and fallow fields.—**SVC and WVB**—with winter quarters in Western Europe and as far south as North Africa.—**Food:** Vegetarian as all other geese. On land they feed on fodder, grasses and sedges, but they also eat herbs and shrubs, and seasonally also green stuff, roots, seeds and tubers.—**Nesting:** Breed on the ground; the soft warm nest lined with down mainly on old rushes and reed-beds, in undergrowth, and even in the open. Lays 3-14 eggs, though usually 4-9. Incubation period lasts 28-29 days; the goslings leave the nest after being hatched and they are able to fly when 10 weeks old, but they remain with the family until the following spring.

Mallard

Anas platyrhynchos

Drakes of many duck species are adorned throughout almost the entire year with a colourful plumage which contrasts with the plain brown plumage of the ducks. Only in summer and early autumn does the drake's resemble that of the duck. The surface-feeding ducks of the Anas genus pair in their winter quarters or during the spring migration. The drake follows the duck to its home. In all seasons the Mallard is the most frequently seen species. Mallards are the progenitors of our domestic ducks.—**Characteristics:** Male in nuptial plumage has a dark green head which is separated from the dark-brown breast by a white neck-ring; feet orange-red. Female speckled brown, bill greenish. In flight both birds' characteristic metal-blue speculum is visible. Females and juveniles **may** easily **be confused with** many other surface feeding ducks.—**Habitat:** On all waters in town and countryside.—**PB.**—**Food:** Variable according to seasons; in late autumn, winter and early spring almost exclusively vegetarian (seeds and winter shoots); in breeding-time and early summer predominantly molluscs and insects.—**Nesting:** Breeds on the ground and occasionally in holes in trees; they usually contain 7-11 eggs; incubation period 24-32 days. Female leads the young until they are capable of flying at 8 weeks of age.

Pintail

Anas acuta

Characteristics: Male in nuptial plumage, a brown head and neck with a stiletto-shaped streak continuing the white of the throat, a long black needle-pointed tail, flank and upper parts grey. Female striped light-brown. Bill of both birds lead-grey. Drake's wing speculum is green, the duck's an indistinct rust-brown.—**May be confused with** the same birds as the Mallard (see above).—**Habitat:** On large lakes rich in vegetation, bogs, moors and downs. During passage and in winter in estuaries, lagoons and along the sea coast. Breeds in parts of north-eastern Europe—**PB.**—**Food:** Seasonally changeable as in the case of the Mallard. Looks for food in shallow inland lakes and on the sea shore.—**Nesting:** Breeds on moors, lake islands, marshes and occasionally sand dunes. Normally it lays 7-11 eggs; incubation period 21-23 days. Female leads the ducklings until they can fly at the age of 7 weeks.

Tufted Duck

Aythya fuligula

Diving ducks of the Aythya genus dive and swim under water in contrast to the surface ducks which "duck" (Heads in the water, tails in the air). Diving ducks are also more squat and lie more deeply in the water.—**Characteristics:** Male in nuptial plumage, black with white flanks, head shimmering purple-violet with a tuft on the back of the head. Female and young birds are a blackish brown; females in winter plumage have a narrow white bill base, and belly and vent region varying from white to black.—**May be confused with** the Scaup; but male Tufted smaller and has tuft, and female tufted has no white ring around base on bill as female Scaup. The Scaup breeds in parts of Scandinavia, but is mostly a winter visitor to Britain and southern Europe.—**Habitat:** Tufted Ducks live on lakes and ponds up to six metres in depth, seldom at sea. Outside the breeding period also on slow flowing waters. Breeds mostly in north and eastern Europe.—**PB.**—**Food:** Chiefly molluscs, also animal and vegetable matter.—**Nesting:** They build their nests on the ground on islets, usually well covered. They lay 5-12 eggs. Incubation period 23-25 days. The female leads the ducklings for 6 weeks; at the age of 9 weeks they are able to fly.

Pochard

Aythya ferina

Characteristics: Male in nuptial plumage has a reddish brown head and neck, breast and rump are black, flanks and back grey. The female is dark brown, flanks and back grey with fine dark bars. Females **may be confused with** those of the Tufted Ducks (as above) and Scaups, but can be distinguished from them by the faded light-brown patch on chin and bill base, and by the brown eyes instead of yellow.—**Habitat:** Much the same as Tufted Duck. Breeds in north and eastern Europe.—**PB.**—**Food:** Plant and animal matter of all kinds, from the smallest fly larvae to larger plants.—**Nesting:** Breeds on the ground; it builds its nest near water in reeds or riverbank. It lays 6-9 eggs. Incubation period lasts 23-28 days. The female leads the young for 50-55 days.

Goshawk

Accipiter gentilis

Characteristics: Bird of prey the size of a Buzzard. Its entire under-parts closely barred dark brown. Vertical down-strokes (viz. picture) produce a criss-cross pattern. Its long rounded tail (the Sparrow Hawk's tail is square) has four dark bands. Upper parts dark grey-brown to slate grey, also cheeks. Above the light red eyes it has a broad white eye stripe. Male smaller than female. Young Goshawks look totally different; they are medium brown with dark brown longitudinal stripes on a beige background on their under-parts. Their eyes are yellow.—**May be confused with** the Sparrow Hawk (see below). It needs a lot of experience to differentiate between the two species when birds are in flight. Both have broad rounded wings.—**Habitat:** Richly varied wood and farmland. Needs cover. Very rare in Britain, breeding only in continental Europe.—**PC.**—**Food:** Birds and mammals, often jays, wood-pigeons, thrushes and rabbits.—**Nesting:** Nests in the tops of high forest trees. Clutch consists usually of 3-4 eggs; incubation period 35-42 days; nestlings leave after 36-40 days.

Sparrow Hawk

Accipiter nisus

Characteristics: A bird of prey, female size of pigeon, male smaller. Under-parts barred, rusty-brown in case of male, female grey; male's upper-parts blue-grey to slate grey, female browner. The long square tail has four bands across, as that of the Goshawk. Male's cheeks rusty brown; only the females and juveniles have a white supercilium which is smaller than that of the Goshawk. Eyes yellow to orange-red (in the old male), and narrower than that of Goshawk. Juveniles resemble the parent birds more than do the Goshawk's and are browner.—**May be confused with** the Goshawk (see above).—**Habitat:** Open woodland and farmland with hedges.—**PB.**—**Food:** Small birds which it out-flies. Hunts with lightning speed and skill along hedges.—**Nesting:** Nests in trees, preferably firs. Clutch of 4-6 eggs. Incubation period 33-36 days; young leave nest after 24-30 days.

Buzzard

Buteo buteo

Characteristics: A large strong bird of prey with a short, but broad, narrowly barred tail. Upper-parts medium to dark brown, the rest of the plumage varies greatly. There are buzzards with nearly white to dark-brown under-parts. Characteristic soaring flight. With the Kestrel our most frequently seen bird of prey in fields and woodlands, but predominantly in wilder country, moors etc. It calls often with its well-known mewing sound.—**May be confused with** the Honey Buzzard, *Pernis apivorus* (summer visitor) which is, however, slenderer, has longer wings and only three broad dark bars across its tail, one at the end and two near legs; with a rare winter visitor, the Rough-Legged Buzzard, *Buteo lagopus,* whose white tail-underside ends in a dark broad bank; and with Kites (see below) which have forked tails.—**Habitat:** Over open country.—**PB.**—**Food:** Voles as well as other small mammals, young birds, reptiles, insects and carrion.—**Nesting:** Nests in trees; lays 2-3 eggs; incubation period 33-35 days; young birds leave nest after 42-49 days.

Black Kite

Milvus migrans

Kites are buzzard-sized slender birds of prey with long wings and a forked tail. Present-day total waste disposal methods have greatly reduced the basis of the Black Kite's existence as they are scavengers, and the reduction in their numbers has thus probably directly increased the pollution of our waters. Noisy.—**Characteristics:** Tail of the dark brown Black Kite—not seen in Britain, but common over the Swiss lakes, for instance—is only slightly forked and has distinct dark transverse bars; seen in flight under-parts almost uniformly blackish-brown. Red Kites *(Milvus milvus)*—very rare—are a lighter brown, and have a distinct long forked tail, the upper side of which is uniformly rusty-red and the lower side light beige.—**May be confused with** buzzards (see above) and harriers. However, only the kites have forked tails.—**Habitat:** Woodlands near lakes and rivers. Black Kite **SVC.** Red Kite **PB.**—**Food:** Fish clawed from the water surface; birds, carrion, small mammals.—**Nesting:** Breeds in trees in forests; usually lays 2-3 eggs. Incubation about 28 days. Young leave nest after 42-52 days (Red Kite nestlings after 40-60 days).

Hobby

Falco subbuteo

Falcons are small birds of prey with pointed wings and long narrow tails which equip them excellently for their dashing aerial hunting. Their eyes are dark. The females are bigger than the males. They do not build nests of their own.—**Characteristics:** Upper-parts blackish slate-coloured, under-parts heavily streaked lengthwise, with rust-coloured trousers. The black ear-coverts contrast with the white of throat and cheeks. Yellow legs. Juveniles browner without rust-coloured trousers.—**Habitat:** In open woodland up to altitudes of 1,000 metres maximum; also in town parks. Frequent in some localities, absent in others.—**SVB.**—**Food:** Small birds and to a lesser extent insects. In its winter quarters feeds on insects, chiefly termites.—**Nesting:** Breeds in trees, prefers conifers and crows' nests; lays 2-4 eggs. Incubation period 28 days; nestlings leave after 28-32 days.

Kestrel

Falco tinnunculus

This is our hovering "motor-way" falcon.—**Characteristics:** Upper-parts reddish-brown with blackish-brown primaries. Long dark ear-coverts. Under-parts brown longitudinal stripes on a mud-coloured background. Legs yellow. Male crown, neck, ear-coverts and rump a bluish grey, also its tail which has a broad black terminal band. Female reddish-brown wherever the male is grey; tail has narrow dark-brown bars.—**May be confused with** the Lesser Kestrel, *Falco naumanni* which breeds in extreme southern Europe. The two are very much alike. However, the male Lesser Kestrel's upper-parts are not spotted and it does not have long ear-coverts; female has only a suggestion of long ear-coverts. Voices differ considerably. Claws of Lesser Kestrel are light, rarely as dark as those of the Hobby.—**Habitat:** Over open country with no or low vegetation, such as fields, pastures, fallow land, in town and countryside.—**PB.**—**Food:** Mice; where these are lacking it preys on small birds; in towns, on sparrows. It is a hovering hunter.—**Nesting:** Breeds in trees, rocks, buildings (especially in high towers) openly or in crevices. It lays 4-6 eggs; incubation period 27-31 days; young leave nest after 27-38 days.

Pheasant

Phasianus colchicus

Large chicken-like bird, with a very long tail of Asian origin. Male spectacularly gaudy. Many wild birds have, in fact been hand-reared for shooting.—**Characteristics:** Hens are mottled buff and blackish brown; the cocks multi-coloured with long tail. Plumage copper-red, the individual feathers rimmed bluish-black; head metallic green, the naked face blood-red; some cocks white-ringed neck (influence of East-Asian strains). Cocks have a rough loud call. Juveniles have similar colouring as hens and short tails.—**Habitat:** Well-covered farm and park land, woods rich in undergrowth (original habitat).—**PB.**—**Food:** Every kind of vegetable food; small animals ranging up to mice.—**Nesting:** Polygamous: Breeds on the ground; lays 6-12 eggs. Incubation period 22-24 days; chicks leave nest and are able to fly at the age of 10-12 days; the hen leads the chicks until they are 70-80 days old.

Partridge

Perdix perdix

A small chicken-like field-bird living in pairs or in coveys, active also at dusk.—**Characteristics:** When people approach it closely flies up with penetrating calls and falls down after a brief low flights to continue its escape on foot. Upper-parts mottled brown; short rufous tail, face orange-brown. Cocks have a horse-shoe shaped shield on the belly which the hens have only in a faintly defined form or lack entirely.—**Habitat:** Lives on farmland, fields and meadows, favouring warm and dry ground.—**PB.**—**Food:** Green stuff, corn grains, weed seeds, insects. Chicks receive almost exclusively animal food up to four weeks old.—**Nesting:** Nest built in hollow on ground containing usually 10-20 eggs. Incubation period 24-26 days. Fledglings leave nests and are able to fly when 13-14 days old. Chicks are led by both parent birds and remain with them until winter.

Moorhen

Gallinula chloropus

Rails and Moorhens are species' adapted to life in marshes and water. They are bad fliers with short wings and tails. Some of them are adroit divers. Moorhens have become familiar park birds.—**Characteristics:** Pillar-box red frontal shield and bill. Plumage dark grey-black with a thin white streak along flanks. Legs green. Tail white underneath and frequently cocked. Juveniles greyish-brown with beige throat. Young moorhens **may be confused with** young coots (see below) which, however, lack the white under-tail coverts.—**Habitat:** Marshy and muddy banks of inland waters, even very small ones. Favours dense lush vegetation.—**PB.**—**Food:** Variable according to season. Plants and animals of the shore region, under and on the water, in winter also grass.—**Nesting:** Nest usually built concealed on ground, in shrubs and even in trees; in municipal park nest may stand totally unconcealed. It lays 5-11 eggs; two broods are usual, the maximum incubation period is 17-24 days. Fledglings leave nest and are able to fly after roughly 35 days. Family remains together longer.

Coot

Fulica atra

A species of rail adapted to swimming and diving. Familiar on lakes and rivers and large ponds in towns.—**Characteristics:** A pitch-black bird with a white frontal shield and bill. Colour of the partially webbed feet varies from leaden grey to yellow. Juveniles resemble young moorhens but lack their white under-tail coverts.—**Habitat:** Still and slow flowing waters, rich in food, extending over an area of more than 100 sq. metres and with shallow overgrown banks; also in park ponds.—**P.B.**—**Food:** Plants and animal matter on banks, on and under water. Coots are able to duck and dive, pick up and graze. They feed predominantly on aquatic plants, small molluscs and water insects.—**Nesting:** Nests in dense riparian vegetation in water and lays 5-10 eggs. Second broods have been known in individual cases. Incubation period 22-24 days. Fledglings leave nest and are able to fly at about 8 weeks.

Oystercatcher

Haematopus ostralegus

A common bird of the coast, conspicuous by its black and white appearance. Noisy. Actually lives on molluscs not oysters.—**Characteristics:** About the size of a Wood Pigeon, black head, breast and back, white belly, white wing-bar, and black and white tail. Large orange bill and pinkish legs. Sexes the same. Voice a loud piping, often sustained.—**May be confused with** Avocet, *Recurvirostra avosetta* (scarce summer visitor to Britain) and with Black-winged Stilt, *Himantopus himantopus* (summer visitor to southern Europe, rare in Britain).—**Habitat:** Sea shores, estuaries, sometimes on inland water (especially in north Britain).—**PB.**—**Food:** Limpets, mussels, cockles, sometimes marine crustacea etc.—**Nesting:** rudimentary nest on shingle, dunes, grass near water; lays usually 2-4 eggs; incubation period 24-27 days; young leave nest after about two days, tended by both parents.

Lapwing or Peewit

Vanellus vanellus

Among the plovers the Lapwing is by far the most frequent inland breeder and the one the amateur is most likely to meet and notice.—**Characteristics:** Black and white bird, the size of a pigeon, whose dark plumage has a metallic purple and green lustre. It has a long crest, broad rounded wings, and a white tail with broad black terminal band. It is identifiable by its flapping display and territorial defence flights and by its call "pee-witt".—**Habitat:** Large flat stretches of land with little or no vegetation such as meadows, ploughlands, marshes, downs and fallow ground.—**PB.**—**Food:** All kinds of small ground animals which it entices out by tapping the ground, grubbing them out and picking them up.—**Nesting:** Nests in a self-made hollow, usually in ploughland fields, lays 4 eggs. Incubation period 26-29 days. Fledglings leave nest and fly when 30-42 days old.

Black-headed Gull

Larus ridibundus

The bold and adaptable Black-headed Gull has been making increasing use of the special sources of floating waste food in our towns and of the people willing to feed it. It has now become a familiar and frequent winter visitor to our towns, and most of the gulls seen in built-up areas are Black-headed.—**Characteristics:** A typical white gull with black wing-tips and specific white wing fore-edges visible in flight. In winter head white with dark patch behind ear; in summer chocolate-brown with white eye-ring. Bill and legs a deep red. Juveniles have patterned brown wings and back of the head, and a black terminal band on tail. Dark bill, legs flesh-coloured.—**Habitat:** Near all kinds of water, on coasts and in towns; when breeding found near inland waters rich in food.—**PB.**—**Food:** All kinds of small animals, mice, human refuse.—**Nesting:** Breeds in colonies on inaccessible islands, marshes, moors etc. Nest built on ground containing usually 3 eggs. Incubation period 21-27 days; fledglings leave nest after 2-3 days and fly when 5 weeks old.

Common Gull

Larus canus

Characteristics: A medium-large white gull, with greenish-yellow legs and bill, black wing tips marked with white. In winter crown and neck streaked greyish-brown. Tail white with broad black terminal band. Juveniles dark brown, as the young of all large gulls, flesh-coloured bill with brown tip, and flesh-brown legs.—**May be confused with** Herring Gull.—**Habitat:** After the Black-headed and Herring Gull the most often seen inland gull, but predominantly a coastal bird.—**PB.**—**Food:** All kinds of ground animals up to the size of voles, frogs and young birds, carrion, human refuse.—**Nesting:** Breeds colonially on coastal land in north and north-eastern Europe. Also now inland, on lonely moors and fallow land. Ground nest containing 2-3 eggs. Incubation period 22-29 days, fledglings leave nest after 2-3 days and are able to fly aged 5 weeks.

Herring Gull

Larus argentatus *see p. 144*

Woodpigeon

Columba palumbus

Pigeons are an ancient family of grain and fruit eating birds. They do not drink by lifting their heads but suck up the water as through a straw. When sitting on eggs males and females alternate at fixed times. They are the only birds which feed their young with so-called pigeon milk produced in the crop lining of both parent birds. Shy, and "clatter" when disturbed from trees.—**Characteristics:** A big strong blue-grey pigeon with pure white patches on neck and white crescent-shaped bands on wings. Green and purple tinged feathers surround the white neck patches. Patches absent in juveniles. Typical "cooing" song.—**May be confused with** the Stock Dove, *Columba oenas* (found scattered throughout Europe) which is smaller than the Woodpigeon, white absent from neck and wing; with the Rock Dove, *Columba livia* (to be seen on rocky sea cliffs in Britain, and inland cliffs in continental Europe), also smaller, with white rump and two marked black wing-bars, the precursor of our town pigeon; and with feral pigeons, which vary very much but also lack white markings.—**Habitat:** Woods, town parks and gardens, clearings, cultivated areas wherever it can find food.—**PB.**—**Food:** Grain, seeds of all kinds, buds, delicate green stuff, cabbage. Seasonally changeable.—**Nesting:** Nests in trees, 2 broods a year, in towns more broods; lays 2 eggs; incubation period 15-18 days; fledglings leave nest at 3-4 weeks of age.

Collared Dove

Streptopelia decaocto

In a spectacular advance, the Collared Dove, which originated in the Balkans and Southern Asia, has overrun Central and Western Europe.—**Characteristics:** Small unspotted grey-brown pigeon with a characteristic black crescent, rimmed white, on the neck. Crescent absent in juveniles. Characteristic three "coo's", second one accentuated.—**May be confused with** Turtle Dove (p. 42).—**Habitat:** Towns, villages, cultivated areas.—**PB.**—**Food:** Food of domestic animals, refuse, seeds, green stuff, berries, small animals.—**Nesting:** Nests in trees and buildings; 3-5 broods a year. The slovenly nest contains 2 eggs; incubation period 14-17 days, fledglings leave nest after 17-20 days.

Turtle Dove

Streptopelia turtur

Characteristics: A small brown-coloured pigeon, upper-parts spotted, with black and white striped neck patch. Breast wine-red, back rufous. Neck patches absent in juveniles. Characteristic song soft and purring.—**May be confused with** Collared Dove (p. 40) which is completely unspotted and has a crescent-shaped mark instead of the neck patches.—**Habitat:** In open woodland. As it needs warmth it is not to be found everywhere. Prefers plains and valleys open to a southern aspect up to 1,000 metres in altitude.—**SVB.**—**Food:** Seeds of all kinds, buds, greenery, berries.—**Nesting:** The slovenly flimsy nest containing two eggs well hidden in trees and thick hedges. Possibly two broods a year in the South. Incubation period 13-15 days, fledglings leave nest after 14-16 days.

Cuckoo

Cuculus canorus

Everyone has heard the Cuckoo, but few have seen it. Yet is not particularly shy but more inconspicuous owing to its grey-brown plumage and its mode of life. In large areas of open country it sits freely on fences and cables.—**Characteristics:** A medium-sized grey and relatively slender bird with a white belly with grey crosswise bars. In its brown phase the female is also barred on upper-parts. Eyes orange-red. Its characteristic echoing cuckoo call is heard from early May until about end July.—**May be confused with** the Sparrow Hawk (p. 26) and female Kestrel (p. 30). But the shape of its bill is quite different and its grey rounded tail with delicate white longitudinal spots unmistakable.—**Habitat:** Areas with dotted trees, and also quite open ground. Also moors, heaths, edges of woodlands.—**SVB.**—Winters in South and East Africa.—**Food:** Hairy caterpillars which other birds scorn, insects, spiders, earthworms.—**Nesting:** Our only bird that lays its eggs in the nests of other song-birds which incubate and raise them. According to region it uses very different host birds and lays one egg at a time into the alien nest and removes one host egg. A female cuckoo lays about 10 eggs a year. At the age of 1-4 days the young cuckoo levers the young of the host parents out of the nest. Incubation periods 12 days, leaves nest after 21-23 days. The foster-parents lead the young cuckoo for another 3 weeks.

Barn Owl

Tyto alba

Owls are nocturnal carnivorous birds, with extremely good vision and hearing which helps them to hunt at night and in twilight conditions. The big eyes are situated in front and not at the side of the head as with other birds. The head is very mobile. Owing to their soft plumage owls fly noiselessly. They vomit indigestible matter, such as bones and hairs in sausage-shaped pellets.—**Characteristics:** The Barn Owl is the only owl without stripes. At best it is delicately speckled on its white, cream-coloured or yellow-brown under-parts (2 colour forms). Its upper-parts are golden yellow with dark-brown mottling. Heart-shaped mask-like face. No ear-tufts. Voice distinguished from Little Owl (p. 44) and Tawny Owl (p. 46) by its sustained shriek-like call.—**Habitat:** Hunts over open fields and meadows, roosts in church towers, barns, old buildings; found in altitudes up to 800 metres, but not so common since the extensive use of pesticides.—**PB.**—**Food:** Predominantly voles, also shrews; in addition birds and frogs.—**Nesting:** Nests in farm buildings, abandoned ruins. Lays 4-7 eggs; 2 broods in years when mice are plentiful, none when scarce. Incubation period 30-40 days, fledglings leave at age of 7-9 weeks.

Little Owl

Athene noctua

In ancient Greece the Little Owl, a sacred bird, accompanied Pallas Athene, goddess of wisdom. Another western race was introduced into Britain towards the end of the last century.—**Characteristics:** A small short-tailed squat owl which if often seen during the day on roofs, fences, posts etc. Big shining yellow eyes look out from under domed forehead. Its bill is almost level with its eyes. Upper-parts of plumage dark-brown with buff specks, under-parts light buff-coloured with dark-brown longitudinal stripes. A shrill cry, as well as staccato barking.—**Habitat:** Hunts in orchards, fruit plantations, pastures, gardens, forest edges and deserted moorland up to an altitude of about 600 metres.—**PB.**—**Food:** Mice and insects, above all beetles.—**Nesting:** Nests in natural tree hollows and in attics; accepts nesting boxes; lays 3-6 eggs; incubation period 28-29 days; fledglings leave nest at 4-5 weeks of age.

Tawny Owl

Strix aluco

From earliest times owls have excited man's imagination because of their soundless flight, mysterious calls and nocturnal life. Good and evil have been attributed to them. The shrill "kewick" of the Tawny Owl pictured here was regarded by many as the call of the bird of death. In fact we should be grateful to them for their ceaseless hunting of mice, and protection of them is essential.—**Characteristics:** A large squat owl with brownish-black eyes in the middle of its face just above the base of the bill. A dark stripe in the middle of the crown goes down to the eyes. Appears in 2 colour phases, grey and brown. Adult birds have longitudinal streaks ending crosswise. Juveniles have transverse bands everywhere. No ear-tufts. Loudest of owls described here. A quick two-note call, as well as well known resonant tu-whit-tu-woo.—**Habitat:** Hunts skilfully in shrubs and woods. Roosts in old forests, parks, cemeteries and tree-lined roads; up to an altitude of 1,800 metres.—**PB.**—**Food:** Catches every animal ranging in size from beetles to rats and coots. Mice and voles predominate. The young are given a lot of earthworm.—**Nesting:** Breeds in the old nests of crows and birds of prey, and in hollow trees. Lays usually 2-5 eggs; incubation period 28-30 days; fledglings leave nest aged 4-5 weeks.

Long-eared Owl

Asio otus

Owls fly swiftly and very silently, and in twilight it is often quite difficult to identify them. In poor light, relative size is one of the best guides, as are their call notes. Owls can often be studied whilst roosting in daytime, if one approaches them cautiously.—**Characteristics:** A medium-sized slender owl with beautiful ear-tufts, yellow to orange-coloured eyes and brown plumage resembling bark. Under-parts longitudinal streaks and cross-barring. Above each eye a light triangle; base of bill below eyes. Voice a low "oo-oo-oo", less harsh than Tawny Owl.—**May be confused with** the Short-eared Owl, *Asio flammeus* (scattered in Europe) though its ear tufts are not easily visible; the rare Eagle Owl, *Bubo bubo,* a thick-set, strong almost eagle-sized owl whose ear-tufts begin directly above the eyes and whose dark-spotted crown stretches down to the eyes. The base of the bill is higher than that of the Long-eared Owl, and the white triangle is absent. It is twice the size of the Long-eared Owl.—**Habitat:** Favours conifer woods, above all firs; found also in cemeteries and parks. Hunts in open land, ploughed fields, meadows, clearings. Hunts predominantly from concealed position. Long-eared owls can occasionally be seen roosting communally in winter on tree branches.—**PB.**—**Food:** Much of its prey consists of voles but also other small mammals, birds up to thrush-size and beetles.—**Nesting:** Nests in old nests of crows and magpies, preferably in conifers, sometimes on ground. Lays 3-7 eggs. Sometimes no brood in years when mice are scarce. Incubation period 27-29 days; fledglings leave nest after 20-26 days.

Nightjar

Caprimulgus europaeus

The Roman writer, Pliny the Elder, maintained 2,000 years ago that the Nightjar milked goats. This explains the Latin name of this strange nocturnal bird. During the day it sleeps, invisible, on the ground, on tree stumps or lengthways on branches. Its day begins at about sunset and ends well before sunrise. It is identified by its remarkable churring song.—**Characteristics:** Even seasoned ornithologists hardly ever see it in day-time as its brown and grey plumage so deceptively resembles tree-bark. It is about the size of a Mistle Thrush, has long pointed wings and a long tail. The male has a large white patch at the tip of the two outer tail feathers. Its loud monotonous churring song performed in flight or in repose can be heard during warm nights from May on.— **Habitat:** On dry sunny commons and woodland glades.—**SVB.**—Winters mainly in South Africa.—**Food:** Nocturnal insects caught and eaten on wing.—**Nesting:** Lays 2 eggs on bare ground. Incubation period 17-18 days, fledglings leave after 15-19 days; 2 overlapping broods per year.

Swift

Apus apus

In summer we recognise the arrival of the Swift when we hear its typical shrill screaming and see its rapid dashing flight.—**Characteristics:** Brown-black plumage, long sickle-shaped wings. Short weak feet.—**May be confused with** swallows (p. 60) though they do not fly as fast, nor do they scream or have scythe-shaped wings.—**Habitat:** In the air, in bad weather skimming just above ground and water.—**SVB.**—it spends the winter in Africa.—**Food:** Flying insects; if these are absent, long migrations are undertaken even in the breeding season. The fledglings left behind may be without food for up to nine days.—**Nesting:** Nests very high in chimneys, buildings in town and countryside. Lays 2-3 eggs, incubation period 19-21 days, fledglings leave nest after 40-60 days, according to weather conditions.

Kingfisher
Alcedo atthis

As a resident bird the Kingfisher, with its brilliant tropical appearance, is becoming increasingly rare, not only as a result of icy winters but also because of the thoughtlessness of man. Many breeding places are lost due to the unnecessary clearing and changing of steep stream and river banks and some fish breeders continue to begrudge this splendid bird its insignificant meal of fish. A little consideration would considerably help the species.—**Characteristics:** As a member of a tropical bird family brilliantly colourful. Upper-parts brilliant iridescent blue and green, under-parts chestnut brown. The small feet coral-red, the powerful dagger-shaped bill a dark horn colour. It is a thick-set short-necked and short-tailed sitting hunter with direct, rapid flight. Unsociable.—**Habitat:** Along upper reaches of streams and rivers and ponds. In winter it comes down to marshes and to the sea.—**PB.—Food:** Fish, water insects, horse-leeches, water snails and small amphibians. Fishes only in clean water; need at least one km. of river-course as base for its food.—**Nesting:** Bores long nesting holes in steep firm banks, rarely further afield. Lays usually 6-7 eggs. Incubation period 19-21 days, fledglings leave nest after 23-27 days; at times 2-3 broods a year.

Woodpeckers
Picidae

This ancient well-defined bird family is excellently adapted to its arboreal way of life. They are able to climb the steep surfaces of the trunks with the help of their claw formation and their still tail which is used as a prop; the chisel-bill and head equipped with shock absorbers enable them to drill holes into hard wood in order to find food, and also to produce their characteristic resonant drumming noise on trunks; and the extremely long arrow-shaped tongue acts like a sticky harpoon which enables the bird to get caterpillars, larvae and insects eggs out of the smallest and deepest holes. Woodpeckers are unsocial forest inhabitants. The Woodpecker species' to be seen in Britain and in continental Europe are mainly resident except the Wryneck, which is a migrant. The woodpeckers make their own nest holes.

Black Woodpecker

Dryocopus martius

Characteristics: It is the largest European woodpecker, the size of a crow. Deep black with light horn-coloured bill. Male with red crown, female only a red patch at the back of the head. Eyes light yellow. Characteristic loud call notes. Drums.—**Habitat:** Not found in Britain, but resident in northern and eastern Europe. Large forests with high trees. Covers large territories of 400 to 800 hectares. The only enemies of this strong bird are the Goshawk and the Marten.—**PC.**—**Food:** Insects living in timber; ants, seeds of conifers.—**Nesting:** Lays 3-6 eggs. Incubation period 12-14 days. Fledglings leave nest after 24-28 days.

Great Spotted Woodpecker

Dendrocopos major   *photographed on p. 57 lower left*

The Great Spotted Woodpecker is the most frequent and the most widely distributed species of the five European black and white patterned woodpeckers. We mention here also the Middle-Spotted Woodpecker, *Dendrocopos medius,* and the Lesser Spotted Woodpecker, *Dendrocopos minor.*—**Characteristics:** Great Spotted Woodpecker: Black crown; male has crimson nape patch, white cheeks with black bar, crimson under-tail coverts, white wing-shields, longer than those of the Middle-Spotted. Juveniles have red crown. Drums. Middle-Spotted Woodpecker: Both sexes the same; crown red, unrimmed; white cheeks without centre bar; pale-red under-tail coverts; its white wing shields shorter than those of Great Spotted; almost equal size. Lesser spotted Woodpecker: Sparrow-sized; upper-parts black and white cross-barred; male black rimmed red crown; female black crown without any red; cheeks without bar. Drums.—**Habitat:** Woods, parks and gardens. Middle-Spotted (not in Britain, but in central and south-eastern Europe) only in deciduous woods. Lesser Spotted favours flat landscapes. Great Spotted—**PB.**—Middle-Spotted—**PC.**—Lesser Spotted—**PB.**—**Food:** Great Spotted (pecks and drills) insects, seeds, spiders and berries. Middle-Spotted (drills) beetles, preferably ants, and in winter, seeds. Lesser Spotted: (drills) aphis, ants, preferably beetles.—**Nesting:** Great Spotted: 4-8 eggs; incubation 8-11 days; fledglings nidicolous for 20-24 days. Middle-Spotted: usually 5-6 eggs; incubation 11-12 days; fledglings nidicolous 20-23 days. Lesser Spotted: Usually 4-6 eggs; incubation 11-12 days, fledglings nidicolous 18-23 days.

Grey-headed Woodpecker

Picus canus

Green Woodpecker

Picus viridis

Characteristics: Green Woodpecker: Entire crown, in male also nape, crimson; eyes black-rimmed, broad pronounced moustachial stripe in female black, in male red with black surround. Juveniles' under-parts have brown wavy bars. Grey-headed Woodpecker: Head and crown grey, has red forehead; narrow black cheek stripe; near the eye a black streak running to the bill. Juveniles brownish with barred under-parts. Grey Woodpeckers like to drum, Green Woodpeckers drum only exceptionally. Green Woodpecker noted for typical loud echoing "laugh", hence the common name in Britain is yaffle. Grey-headed similar call, but less harsh. Both species **may be confused.—Habitat:** Green Woodpecker common in Britain, not in Scotland or Ireland; the Grey-headed principally in central continental Europe, eastwards and parts of north, but not in Britain. Deciduous woods, parks; Green Woodpecker also in gardens. Grey-headed.—**PC.**—Green—**PB.**—**Food:** Green Woodpecker feeds almost exclusively on ants it picks up on the ground and in their subterranean nests. Grey-headed Woodpecker: not known for certain, most likely ants and insects.—**Nesting:** Green Woodpecker: Usually 5-6 eggs; incubation period 14-20 days; fledglings nidicolous 19-27 days. Grey-headed Woodpecker: Usually 6-7 eggs; incubation 17-18 days, fledglings nidicolous 24-25 days.

Wryneck *Jynx torquilla* *photographed lower right*

A strange woodpecker with plumage as soft as that of an owl. Its sticky tongue is not barbed. Its name describes the twisting, threatening head movements when on the look-out or displaying.—**Characteristics:** It is the size of a finch and its plumage looks like tree bark. Under-parts lighter and closely variegated in brown and grey. Delicate bill and strong feet. It utters characteristic loud sequences of call-notes.—**Habitat:** It is very scarce in Britain, only found in a small part of Southern England. In woods and copses, parks and gardens. It is fond of light and warmth.—**SVB.**—winters in tropical Africa north of the equator.—**Food:** Almost exclusively ants which it finds on the ground and in their subterranean nests.—**Nesting:** The only woodpecker which does not make its own nesting hole. It looks for one and ruthlessly evicts any inhabitants. Accepts nest-boxes readily. Lays usually 7-11 eggs; incubation 12-14 days; fledglings nidicolous 19-24 days.

56

Song Birds

The large order of song birds inhabits all types of landscapes from mountain tops down to the sea shore. They are all perching birds, and also have in common the ability to sing. The male makes use of the song to define the limits of its territory, to defend it and to attract a mate. Only a few genera, such as the crows, have no song of their own. But they are very well able to imitate other songs and noises including human sounds. Song birds build their own nests. In this the participation of the sexes varies from species to species. All song birds are nidicolous and are born blind.

Sky Lark

Alauda arvensis

Larks are brown ground-birds which sing their often lovely song on the wing. Among the three larks which breed in Europe only the Sky Lark is found frequently and everywhere.—**Characteristics:** Like all our larks its upper-parts are streaked dark-brown all over, under-parts grey-white. Throat has brown longitudinal stripes. Specific for the species are the white outer-tail feathers. Noted for sustained song, very musical and loud, which it delivers when hovering high up, ascending and descending.—**May be confused with** the Crested Lark, *Galerida cristate* (continental Europe, but rare Britain) and the Wood Lark, *Lullula arborea* (only southern half Britain, but most of continental Europe). Both lack the white tail-feathers and inhabit different landscapes. Also with Pipits.—**Habitat:** Farmland, most frequently in corn fields, meadows, marshes and high heathland. Owing to excessive and often unnecessary disinfection of seed-corn and careless pest control greatly at risk.—**PB.**—**Food:** Seeds of all kinds, insects, spiders, worms, all of which picked up from the ground.—**Nesting:** Ground-nest with 3-5 eggs; 2 broods per year; incubation period 11-14 days; fledglings leave nest after 9-10 days but fly only when 3 weeks old.

Swallow

Hirundo rustica

The Swallow traditionally heralds the beginning of summer, arriving in Britain April-May. It is a bird of legend and of many wise sayings. Breeding principally in farm buildings, it has become a victim of changed methods of agriculture.—**Characteristics:** Upper-parts brilliant steel-blue, including band round crop; forehead and throat rusty-brown. Under-parts cream coloured; forked tail with two long streamers; shorter in juveniles. Twitters perched on telegraph wires.—**Habitat:** Swooping over roads, houses and every kind of landscape, also over water.—**SVB.**—winters in tropical West Africa and in Congo basin.—**Food:** Flying insects caught on wing.—**Nesting:** Bowl-shaped nest often on rafters with 4-6 eggs; frequently 2 broods a year; incubation period 11-18 days; nestlings nidicolous for 18-23 days.

House Martin

Delichon urbica

Another summer visitor, arriving later than the Swallow: its ball-shaped nests can be seen under the eaves of houses. As it readily accepts artificial nests, one can fix them to buildings with smooth straight wall. It is at risk, like the Swallow.—**Characteristics:** Broad white rump in metallic black upper-parts: under-parts snow-white. Tail only slightly forked. Juveniles brown upper-parts. Twittering song delivered on wing, harsher than Swallow, but less sustained.—**Habitat:** In towns and villages, in high mountains also on rocks. Aerial hunter; hunts usually in higher air layers than Swallow.—**SVB.**—winters in Africa South of the Sahara.—**Food:** Flying insects.—**Nesting:** Globular nest with small opening near top; usually 3-6 eggs; incubation period 12-19 days; nestlings nidicolous for 24-28 days; 2 broods per year possible.

Sand Martin

Riparia riparia

Characteristics: A brown swallow with white under-parts; brown breast band; short tail unforked.—**May be confused with** Swallows (p. 60) because of its breast band, but Swallows are bigger, more sombre, and have long-forked tails multicoloured.—**Habitat:** On steep walls of earth, sand or clay. Digs its nesting holes into the soft top-layer. Breeds rarely in altitudes above 600 metres. Likes to hunt over water, marshes and meadows, but is also found over other open landscapes.—**SVB,**—winters in East and South Africa.—**Food:** Small insects caught in flight.—**Nesting:** Nest at the end of a 60-65 cm long earth hole which it tunnels itself; lays 5-6 eggs; incubation period 12-16 days; nestlings nidicolous for 16-22 days; frequently 2 broods per year.

Pied/White Wagtail

Motacilla alba

The pipits (p. 66) belong to the same family as wagtails. They are all long-legged, slender terrestrial birds which are able to walk and run well but cannot hop. Gregarious when not breeding. Wagtails make a wagging movement with their long tails.—**Characteristics:** The Pied/White Wagtail, our commonest wagtail, lives in the immediate vicinity of man. A distinctive black and white bird. In Britain Pied Wagtail's summer plumage: breast, throat, nape and back are black; forehead, cheeks and under-parts white. Continental race, White Wagtail, in summer similar but grey back. In winter throat is white, breast has black band, thinner in White Wagtail. Juveniles faded grey with black band on throat. Song is a twitter, usually when in flight. Juveniles **may be confused with** young Yellow/Blue-headed Wagtails (p. 64).—**Habitat:** In open farmland wherever it is damp or where water is nearby. Favours vicinity of buildings, breeding in holes in brickwork. On freshly ploughed fields.—**PB.**—**Food:** Insects, spiders, worms and snails which are picked up from the ground or snatched in the air.—**Nesting:** Nest built 50 cm-3 m high in holes of buildings, dams, gnarled trees, under bridges and among rocks. Usually lays 5-6 eggs; incubation period 12-14 days, nestlings nidicolous for 14-15 days; 2 broods per year.

Yellow/Blue-headed Wagtail

Motacilla flava

There are two yellow coloured wagtails in Europe, the Yellow/Blue-headed and the Grey Wagtail. There are a number of races of the former. The yellowest, the Yellow Wagtail, breeds in Britain; the male has a yellow and olive head with a yellow supercilium. In the central European race, called the Blue-headed Wagtail, the male has a bluey-grey crown and cheek with a white supercilium. The entire under-parts of both races are a brilliant yellow. To distinguish the Yellow/Blue-headed from the Grey Wagtail (see below) one must look at the colour of their backs: olive-green in the case of the Yellow/Blue-headed and grey in the case of the Grey Wagtail. It is not easy to distinguish young Yellow/Blue-headed Wagtails from young Pied/White Wagtails. Call-notes loud, squeak-like note.—**Habitat:** A lowland bird favouring meadows, open agricultural land, damp heaths, gravelly soil usually near water.—**SVB,**—winters in West Africa from Senegal to Togoland.—**Food:** Every kind of small animal and flying insects which are caught on short flights or looked for on the ground.—**Nesting:** Nests in depressions on level ground; lays 5-6 eggs; incubation period 12-14 days; nestlings nidicolous for 12-13 days; 2 broods possible.

Grey Wagtail

Motacilla cinerea

Characteristics: A yellow wagtail with a very long tail, a grey back. In nuptial plumage male's throat is black, in winter plumage whitish with a brownish breast; female also has a white throat, brownish breast, its under-parts are a paler yellow and in some birds limited to the under-tail coverts. Juveniles have pure-grey upper-parts, whitish-grey under-parts with yellow under-tail coverts. Call-notes a metallic, somewhat hard "zesit".—**May be confused with** Yellow/Blue-headed Wagtail (see above)—**Habitat:** Lives in pairs along shallow, fast-flowing waters in woods and gorges, also farmland, especially in winter.—**PB.**—**Food:** Small animals found along open river banks. Flying insects near and above water.—**Nesting:** Nests in a hollow near water; lays usually 5-6 eggs; incubation 11-14 days; nestlings nidicolous for 12-13 days; 2 broods per year.

Tree Pipit

Anthus trivialis

Pipits are brown wagtails which are quite difficult to identify. They are typical ground-dwellers, easily mistaken for larks. The expert prefers to identify the four species breeding in Central Europe, and the two or three species which either pass through or winter, on the basis of their voice and song.—**Characteristics:** The Tree Pipit inhabits edges of woods and tree-lined roads and it sings during its fluttering descent from the treetops to the ground.—**May be confused with** the Meadow Pipit (see below) whose song-flight starts on the ground and whose call-notes are different.—**Habitat:** Heaths with scattered trees, clumps of trees, clearings; dry terrain.—**SVB,**—winters in tropical West Africa.—**Food:** Insects, hunts occasionally in flight.—**Nesting:** Nest well-hidden in hollow on ground with 5-6 eggs; incubation period 12-14 days; nestlings nidicolous for 12-14 days; 2 broods a year possible.

Meadow Pipit

Anthus pratensis

Characteristics: A pipit which likes damp terrain and not high trees. It performs its rippling song in a song-flight which it starts from the ground.—**May be confused with** other pipits, particularly with Tree Pipits (see above); on central European mountain meadows with the Water Pipit, *Anthus spinoletta,* which has dark instead of light legs, and with the Rock Pipit, northern European coastal version of Water Pipit. Call-notes identical.—**Habitat:** Damp open landscapes such as meadows, marshes, moors, heaths, waste and fallow land. During winter on fields, near water and on the coast.—**PB.**—**Food:** Insects and some seeds which it picks up from the ground.—**Nesting:** Covered nest on ground with usually 4-6 eggs; incubation period 12-15 days; nestlings nidicolous for 11-14 days; 2 broods per year.

Red-Backed Shrike

Lanius collurio

Shrikes are medium-sized song-birds with hook-tipped bills, hawk-like characteristics, and harsh call-notes. They hunt by patient surveillance from high perches or sometimes by hovering. Surplus food may be impaled on thorns, barbed wire and in forks of branches called "larders". The four species found in Central Europe are at risk and need protection.—**Characteristics:** The Red-Backed Shrike is our smallest shrike. It is the only one breeding in Britain (a summer visitor) and it is now scarce. The male has rufous back and wing coverts, grey head, neck and rump, under-parts cream coloured. Female brown upper-parts, back rufous, under-parts cream-coloured barred with fine crescent-shaped markings on breast and flanks. Juveniles the same colour as female but also with barred upper-parts. Juveniles **may be confused with** young Woodchat Shrikes, *Lanius senator* (not found in Britain).—**Habitat:** On dry open bushy commons, edges of woods, railway embankments, tree nurseries. Favour thorn-hedges.—**SVB,**—winters in East and South Africa. —**Food:** Large insects, caught in flight, predominate in its diet: also frogs, small birds and mice.—**Nesting:** Nests in hedges; lays 4-6 eggs; incubation period 14-16 days; nestlings nidicolous for 12-15 days.

Great Grey Shrike

Lanius excubitor

Characteristics: Largest shrike. Black and grey with white under-parts; light forehead. Juveniles greyish-brown with brown wavy bars on under-parts.—**May be confused with** the rare Lesser Grey Shrike, *Lanius minor,* which only breeds in warmer Southern regions. But this has a black forehead and the white under-parts have a reddish hue.—**Habitat:** Open cultivated country with few trees, high moorland, large wood clearings and orchards.—**PC** and **WVB.**—**Food:** Small vertebrates, particularly voles and insects; birds up to the size of larks as an alternative food, especially in winters with heavy snowfalls.—**Nesting:** Nests in trees, monogamous; lays usually 5-7 eggs; incubation period 17-18 days; nestlings nidicolous for 19-20 days.

Dipper

Cinclus cinclus

Belongs to a small, but very specialised family whose nearest relations are the Wrens. The breeding couples live together in their territories for the whole year and leave only in freezing conditions. They swim and dive extremely well and live near and on water.—**Characteristics:** A stout bird with the round shape of a wren, but larger. Its snow-white bib is sharply separated from the blackish plumage of the rest of the body, sometimes by a rufous stripe. Juveniles' upper-parts slate-grey mottled white, under-parts mottled on whitish grey. The tail is frequently cocked. Sings the whole year.—**Habitat:** Along clear streams and small rivers with stony bottom. Hence it inhabits mountainous and hilly regions. Cautious and shy. One couple needs a river course of 1 km.—**PB.**— **Food:** Water insects, snails, small crawfish, tadpoles, worms. It catches its prey by making a thrusting dive from a perch, into the water, when it often walks upstream underwater; scours river banks.—**Nesting:** It builds a warm globular nest with a small opening and places it between roots on steep inclines, on weirs, mills, under bridges and near waterfalls; lays 5-6 eggs; incubation period 14-18 days; nestlings nidicolous for 19-25 days; 2 broods per year.

Wren

Troglodytes troglodytes

A representative of a family of small brown birds with a remarkably loud voice. Nearest relation is the Dipper.—**Characteristics:** A tiny, plump, lively dark-brown bird with a short cocked tail. Flanks barred. Its strong song is the loudest of all our song-birds. Utter frequent and loud warning calls.—**Habitat:** Undergrowth and thickets in woods, parks and gardens. Must be shady and damp.—**PB.**—**Food:** Insects, spiders, a few berries.—**Nesting:** Builds a number of warm globular nests; sleeps sometimes in one of nests not used for breeding. The male is frequently polygamous. The nest is well-concealed between roots on the ground, in brushwood, wood-stacks, walls. Lays 5-7 eggs; incubation period 14-17 days; nestlings nidicolous for 15-20 days; 2 overlapping broods a year.

Reed Warbler

(opposite)
Acrocephalus scirpaceus

Great Reed Warbler

Acrocephalus arundinaceus

Reed Warblers are inconspicuous insectivorous song-birds with dark-brown upper-parts, cream-coloured under-parts; they live in dense reed, grass or scrub vegetation but can often be easily seen; adept at climbing reed stalks. They are more easily identified by their distinctive song, not by observation. Field ornithologists regard definite identification of these interesting birds as a great achievement. Six species of reed warblers breed in Europe, of which only four species (Great Reed, Reed, Marsh and Sedge Warblers) are generally distributed and frequent.—**Characteristics:** The Reed Warbler has uniformly brown upper-parts, yellow-white lower-parts. Cream-coloured superciliary stripe. Grating voice.—**May be confused with** the Great Reed Warbler which is bigger and has a longer and stronger bill.—**Habitat:** Both of them live in reed-beds, the Great Reed Warbler more towards open water, the Reed Warbler also on banks in osier beds.—Reed Warbler **SVB.**—Great Reed Warbler **SVC.**—Winters in tropical Africa. The third of the reed warbler species, the Sedge Warbler, *Acrocephalus schoenobaenus* (Summer visitor to much of Europe including Britain), lives also in sedges, rushes and osier beds on the banks. It has streaked upper-parts, a striking light superciliary stripe. Its relation, the Aquatic Warbler, *Acrocephalus paludicola* (summer visitor to parts of Europe, but not Britain), has 2 superciliary stripes.—**Food:** Reed Warbler eats small to smallest insects; Great Reed Warbler eats small to medium-sized insects, occasionally small amphibians, in autumn also berries.—**Nesting:** Nest suspended on reeds. Reed Warbler: Lays 3-5 eggs; incubation period 11-14 days; nestlings nidicolous for 11-14 days; 2 broods per year usual. Great Reed Warbler lays 4-6 eggs; incubation period 13-15 days; nestlings nidicolous for 12 days. Both birds are hosts for cuckoos.

Marsh Warbler

Acrocephalus palustris

A reed warbler which does not live in reeds and rushes but in damp weeds, damp brushwood, and also cornfields. Common in central-eastern Europe, but only in south of Britain, locally.—**Characteristics:** As it greatly resembles the Reed and Great Reed Warblers (p. 72) in shape and colour it is identified by its very musical song and habitat. Its rich fluent singing is very varied and full of imitations of the songs of other birds. Sings also at night.—**May be confused with** other reed warblers (p. 72) and by inexperienced bird-watchers also with the Garden Warbler (p. 78) which has brownish-grey upper-parts, but no superciliary stripe. Its song can be mistaken for that of the Icterine Warbler (p. 76).—**Habitat:** Damp weed and shrub thickets, thick hedges, cornfields, sometimes also gardens.—**SVB.**—Travels via Cyprus to its East and South African winter quarters.—**Food:** Insects; in autumn many berries.—**Nesting:** Builds nest suspended on stems or stalks; usually lays 4-5 eggs; incubation period 12-14 days; nestlings nidicolous for 10-14 days.

Dunnock or Hedge Sparrow

Prunella modularis

A slim, secretive insectivorous bird whose colouring resembles that of a sparrow.—**Characteristics:** Back, wings and ears streaked reddish-brown, breast and head grey. Eyes light red-brown, thin bill. Juveniles have streaked under-parts and crown. Pleasant trilling song; resembles muted Wren.—**May be confused with** the House Sparrow (p. 128) female which has, however, the thick bill of a grain-eater and dark brown eyes; also with garden-warblers which are not streaked.—**Habitat:** Woods with much under-growth, hedges, overgrown gardens and parks. Likes shade. In winter it readily makes use of bird-tables and scattered kitchen waste.—**PB.**—**Food:** Looks for food on and near ground. In autumn and winter predominantly seeds, in spring and summer insects, spiders and snails.—**Nesting:** Nests usually low in firs or thick bushes; lays 4-6 eggs; incubation period 11-14 days; nestlings nidicolous for 10-14 days; 2 broods per year.

Icterine Warbler

Hippolais icterina

Tree warblers are related to the reed warblers.—**Characteristics:** Upper-parts greenish-grey; lower-parts yellowish and blue-grey legs.—**May be confused with** smaller leaf warblers (p. 80-3). The Chiffchaff (p. 82), however, has dark legs and grey-white under-parts. The other leaf warblers have light horn coloured legs, moreover their song is entirely different. Its song may be mistaken for that of the Marsh Warbler (p. 74) which also imitates other species' songs.—**Habitat:** In parks, gardens, deciduous and mixed forests rich in under-growth. Prefers the upper half of trees and hedges.—**SVC.**—Winters in Africa south of the Sahara.—**Food:** Small insects which it hunts among the foliage. In autumn also berries.—**Nesting:** Nests in deciduous trees and hedges; lays 4-5 eggs; incubation period 11-14 days; nestlings nidicolous 13-14 days.

Garden Warbler

Sylvia borin

Characteristics: A bird without distinctive features. Upper-parts uniformly brownish olive-grey, under-parts lighter. Brown eyes. Clings to cover. **May** not really **be confused with** any other species, but identification is made more difficult owing to absence of distinctive features. Song unmistakable, sustained and melodious.—**Habitat:** Shady deciduous and mixed forests rich in undergrowth, tree plantations, parks, gardens.—**SVB.**—Winters in tropical West and Central Africa.—**Food:** Soft-skinned insects, fruits.—**Nesting:** Nests usually low down in thickets, brambles, bushes. Lays 3-5 eggs. Incubation period 12-14 days; nestlings nidicolous for 10-12 days; 2 broods a year possible. Popular host for cuckoos.

Blackcap

Sylvia atricapilla

One of our most popular songsters.—**Characteristics:** Very secretive tree warbler, upper-parts grey olive, under-parts grey, with distinctively coloured crown: male black, female and juveniles brown. Hence their name. Their melodious song ends in a full fluting trill.—**Habitat:** As the Garden Warbler and in shady forests with much undergrowth, orchards and commons.—**PB.**—Winters in the Mediterranean region and in tropical Africa.—**Food:** Insects and fruit.—**Nesting:** Small nest built in bushes, evergreens and in stumps of deciduous trees. Lays usually 4-5 eggs; incubation period 12-14 days; nestlings nidicolous for 10-14 days; 2 broods per year.

Lesser Whitethroat

Sylvia curruca (opposite)

Whitethroat

Sylvia communis

Recently the Whitethroat population has dropped dramatically. The causes are probably an excessive use of herbicides along field edges and the southward drift, due to macroclimatic conditions, of the Sahel zone in Africa, the winter quarters of the species.—**Characteristics:** Two small scrub warblers with grey upper-parts, light-grey under-parts and white throats. Difficult to differentiate. However, the Whitethroat has dark-brown wings and light-brown legs, female also brown head. The Lesser Whitethroat, on the other hand, has black cheeks and dark legs. Both are lively birds with horizontal stance. Song of both rattly, Lesser Whitethroat's on one note, Whitethroat's delivered in brief vertical flight.—**May be confused with** other warblers which, however, do not have white outer-tail feathers.—**Habitat:** Whitethroat in open farmland scattered bushes, brambles. Lesser Whitethroat on forest edges, parks, gardens. Both **SVB.**—Whitethroat winters in the Sahel zone, Lesser Whitethroat in North-East Africa.—**Food:** Insects and spiders, caught in bushes, on the ground and in the air; berries.—**Nesting:** Nest in thorn-bushes and hedges. Whitethroat lays 4-6 eggs which it incubates for 11-13 days; nestlings nidicolous for 12 days; 2 broods per year. Lesser Whitethroat nests, as above, and amongst taller vegetation, with trees. Lays 5-6 eggs; incubation 11-14 days; nestlings nidicolous for 12 days.

Wood Warbler

Phylloscopus sibilatrix

Our three leaf warblers (Wood Warbler, Willow Warbler and Chiffchaff) in their respective habitats are common birds which one gets to know quite quickly by their individual songs.—**Characteristics:** The Wood Warbler has green upper-parts with yellow breast and supercilium; throat and belly are white, legs light horn-coloured. Its song is mostly a trill, delivered often high up in trees.—**May be confused with** Willow Warbler (p. 82) and Chiffchaff (p. 82) both of which are smaller; also with Icterine Warblers (p. 76) which has completely yellow under-parts and blue-green legs. The songs of all these species are however totally different.—**Habitat:** Bird of the beech-woods.—**SVB.**—Winters in Africa, South of the Sahara.—**Food:** Insects, spiders in treetops.—**Nesting:** Nests on ground in forests; lays usually 6-7 eggs; incubation period 12-14 days; nestlings nidicolous for 11-12 days.

Willow Warbler

Phylloscopus trochilus

Characteristics: A leaf warbler distinguishable from the Chiffchaff by its light horn-coloured legs and its song. Upperparts grey-green, under-parts grey-white with yellow hue. Yellow supercilium. Its song is a soft descending cadence of whistled tones; melancholic.—**May be confused with** Chiffchaff (see below), which has dark legs, the Wood Warbler (p. 80) which is more yellow and green, and Icterine Warbler (p. 76) whose under-parts are totally yellow and whose legs are blue-grey. All of them have different songs.—**Habitat:** Edges of forests, clearings, copses, marshy woods, river meadows. Needs light and not too dense vegetation.—**SVB.**—Winters in Africa, South of the Sahara.—**Food:** Insects, spiders which it ferrets out in shrubs, picks off leaves and hunts in flight.—**Nesting:** Builds covered nest in hollow on ground; rarely higher; lays 6-7 eggs; incubation period 12-15 days; nestlings nidicolous for 13-16 days.

Chiffchaff

Phylloscopus collybita

The song of this active restless warbler is a repetitive 'chiff chaff'', and gives this Leaf Warbler its name. Common summer visitor.—**Characteristics:** Similar to Willow Warbler; upper-parts olive grey with grey-white under-part. In contrast to Willow and Wood Warblers its legs are blackish brown. The distinctive feature is the song.—**May be confused with** other leaf warblers, and with the Icterine Warbler (p. 76) whose under-parts are yellow and feet leaden-grey.—**Habitat:** In woods with undergrowth, parks and gardens.—**PB.** —Winters in the Mediterranean region and West Africa as far down as 10° North. In autumn it lingers for a long time and some birds winter.—**Food:** Insects and spiders, which are picked off leaves of trees and vegetation. Hunts also flying insects.—**Nesting:** Covered nest near the ground, well concealed in hedges, shrubs and young pines; lays 5-6 eggs; incubation period 13-15 days; nestlings nidicolous for 13-15 days; 2 broods per year.

Goldcrest (Illustrated)

Regulus regulus

Goldcrests and Firecrests are our smallest birds. Although Goldcrests are small they defy winter snows and both species undertake extensive migrations into their winter quarters.—**Characteristics:** An adroit gymnast in the tops of conifers. Upper-parts olive green, under-parts grey-white. Specific features: No white supercilium. The orange-coloured crown, in male, yellow in female, like a middle parting, has a black border. In the males the orange colour is frequently muted so that they are mistaken for females. Head markings absent in juveniles. Low twittering call-note.—**May be confused with** Firecrest (see below).—**Habitat:** Conifer and mixed forests, parks. Particular preference for conifers. In winter often with mixed bands of tits.—**PB.**—**Food:** Small insects and spiders with are picked off needles and branches and chased off branches in a hovering flight. In winter also small seeds.—**Nesting:** A globular matted thickly-walled nest suspended at a height of 10-12 metres from the outer branches of pines or firs. Lays 8-11 eggs; incubation period 12-17 days; nestlings nidicolous for 14-21 days; 2 broods a year.

Firecrest

Regulus ignicapillus

The migration performance of our smallest birds is astonishing. Goldcrests and Firecrests are capable of flying over the Baltic, the North Sea and the Mediterranean.—**Characteristics:** As Goldcrest, but with an additional black eye stripe and white supercilium. Juveniles have only rudimentary eye stripes.—**May be confused with** Goldcrest (see above); song and call-notes different. Call-note of Firecrest is stronger.—**Habitat:** Mixed woods, forests etc. Not as partial to conifers as Goldcrest, but does like certain exotic conifers.—**PC.** and **WVC.**—Breeds in central and southern Europe. Winters south of this, but winter visitor to southern Britain.—**Food:** Small insects, spiders which are picked off branches and needles and caught in flight.—**Nesting:** Suspended nest, but not as high up as Goldcrest; nests also in bushes. Lays 7-11 eggs. Incubation period 12-16 days; nestlings nidicolous 10-20 days; 1-2 broods per year.

Pied Flycatcher

Ficedula hypoleuca

Flycatchers are birds with broad bills which generally hunt insects from a fixed position, catching their prey in the air.—**Characteristics:** In spring head and upper-parts of male black; in autumn, brown as female. Both sexes have distinctive white wing-patch. Outer tail feathers white-edged; male white forehead. Old males have black upper-parts instead of brown.—**May be confused with** Spotted Flycatcher (see below); with Collared Flycatcher, *Ficedula albicollis,* which breeds locally in Southern Europe and whose male is always black and white with an additional broad white neck-ring; female almost indistinguishable from that of Pied Flycatcher.—**Habitat:** In light and sunny woods, parks, avenues and gardens.—**SVB.**—Winters in tropical West and Central Africa.—**Food:** Insects caught in sallies from perching position or picked up from vegetation. Hunts also in fluttering flight. Berries in late autumn.—**Nesting:** Nests in holes in walls and readily accepts nesting boxes. In this way its numbers could be greatly increased. Lays 4-7 eggs; incubation period 12-17 days; nestlings nidicolous for 14-18 days.

Spotted Flycatcher

Muscicapa striata

Characteristics: A quiet unobtrusive greyish-brown bird; crown, throat and breast streaked dark-grey. Without any white at all. Juveniles have grey-spotted under-parts and light-spotted upper-parts. Sits upright and twitches tail and wings frequently.—**May be confused with** Red-breasted Flycatcher (only summer visitor to eastern Europe; extremely rare Britain) which has white wing patches and white-edged outer-tail feathers.—**Habitat:** In light deciduous woods, parks and gardens. Not shy; likes to breed in vicinity of man.—**SVB.**—Winters in the Southern third of Africa.—**Food:** Catches insects in sallies from perch; berries.—**Nesting:** Nest free-standing in forks of branches, in tree-stumps, ivy, on houses, even in flower pots, lays 3-5 eggs; incubation period 12-15 days; nestlings nidicolous for 12-16 days; 2 broods per year.

Stonechat

Saxicola torquata   (above: male   below: female)

The Stonechat and Whinchat belong to the meadow chats. They are small birds inhabiting commons and moors, particularly where there is gorse. Stance upright. They twitch their tails frequently.—**Characteristics:** Male head deep black, upper-parts blackish-brown, white sides of neck and white patch on wing, red-brown breast and white belly; female similar, but head and upper-parts light brown with dark-brown mottling, belly cream-coloured. Call sounds like two stones being banged together.—**May be confused with** Whinchat (p. 90). However, Whinchats have white (male), or cream-coloured (female) supercilium as well as a rufous throat, not black or brown. Thus the Stonechat's head is uniformly coloured and it looks like a hood, whereas in the case of the Whinchat only the crown and the sides of the head are the same colour. Moreover, the Whinchat has a white tail-base.—**Habitat:** On dry sandy soils, hence in railway cuttings, dumps, barren land, poor meadow-land and heaths. During breeding time also on ploughed fields.—**PB.**—**Food:** Either picked up from the ground (Stonechats like to hop) and from grasses and bushes; hunted in horizontal flights over vegetation, or in good weather caught in sally from perch. Insects, spiders, worms, snails.—**Nesting:** Nest very well hidden on ground; lays 4-6 eggs; incubation period 13-14 days; nestlings nidicolous for 14-17 days; 2 broods per year.

Whinchat

Saxicola rubetra

Characteristics: A brown meadow-chat, with white supercilium in male and cream-coloured in female. Two white patches on wings, the second patch being on the primaries. Throat, breast and flanks reddish brown, belly white. Juveniles upper-parts reddish-brown with broad, blackish-brown longitudinal flecks and cream-coloured streaks, underparts cream-coloured. Call a short clicking note. Song not unlike Redstart and Stonechat.—**May be confused with** Stonechat (p. 88) whose head and throat are uniformly coloured, looking like a hood. Juveniles with young Stonechats, whose upper parts are dark brown with cream-coloured longitudinal flecks, and throats brownish.— **Habitat:** Damp pastures and meadows with high vegetation, grass-covered clearings and glades, moorland; also in cultivated fields when migrating.—**SVB.**—Winters in tropical Africa South of the Sahara.—**Food:** As the Stonechat; in addition hunts flying from perch to perch like shrikes.—**Nesting:** Nest is well-hidden on ground; lays 4-6 eggs; incubation period 12-14 days; nestlings nidicolous for 11-14 days.

Redstart

Phoenicurus phoenicurus   (above: male   below: female)

Redstarts are long-tailed, lively and colourful insectivorous
birds.—**Characteristics:** Redstart Males' forehead and belly
white, flanks and breast rufous, upper-parts bluish grey. The
black face mask covers also the throat; no striking wing
markings. Female's upper-parts greyish brown, under-parts
light yellowish-brown, crop greyish-white. Juveniles coloured
like females, scalloped mottling. Song warbler-like, but less
melodious, sounds hurried.—**May be confused with** Black
Redstart (p. 94), in which, however, distribution of white in
male is different and the overall impression of female much
more sombre. Warning calls of both species almost the same;
songs different.—**Habitat:** Light deciduous and mixed
forests, parks.—**SVB.**—winters in the savannas and steppes
of Africa North of Equator.—**Food:** Hunts insects, spiders
and snails on the ground and sometimes snatches prey in
flight; berries.—**Nesting:** Nests in all sorts of holes and
hollows; in trees and buildings as well as in niches in stacked
timber. Lays usually 5-7 eggs; incubation period 12-17 days;
nestlings nidicolous for 13-17 days.

Black Redstart

Phoenicurus ochruros   (above: female   below: male)

The Black Redstart was originally a rock inhabitant but has lived in lowlands for at least 150 years. It found it could live and breed as well on man-made buildings with their many niches as on rock faces.—**Characteristics:** male sooty-black with red rump and tail and white wing-patch. Female, juveniles as well as one-year old males, dark slate-grey with red rump and tail. Song with strained grating and hissing notes. Call-notes like those of Redstart, but somewhat harsher.—**Habitat:** On and near buildings of all kinds. Like to perch on warm roof. In towns and villages, vineyards and high mountain regions.—**PB.**—Only in southern Britain. Breeds in most of Europe, not north; winters westward.—**Food:** Hunts from perches on fences, aerials and telegraph wires for ground and flying insects, wood lice and spiders; berries.—**Nesting:** Nests in all sorts of holes and ledges on houses and walls; lays usually 5-6 eggs; incubation period 13-16 days; nestlings nidicolous for 12-19 days; 2 broods per year.

Nightingale

Luscinia megarhynchos

The Nightingale was venerated in ancient times, for it was considered to be of divine origin. Although its name means night-singer, in reality it is diurnal and sings particularly in the mornings and evenings and sometimes at night. As we know the Marsh Warbler also sings at night. Famous Nightingale song, loud and melodious, notes often repeated. Found now only in southern Britain, as summer visitor.—**Characteristics:** Inconspicuous brown bird with a reddish-brown tail; skulking under cover, and difficult to see.—**May be confused with** its nearest relation, the North-East European Thrush Nightingale, *Luscinia luscinia*. Its song is more monotonous, but no less powerful. It has a brownish mottled breast; and with the female Redstart which lives, however, in open countryside.—**Habitat:** Thick deciduous woods with much undergrowth, bushes and parks.— **SVB.**—Winters in tropical Africa, north of Equator.— **Food:** all kinds of insects and snails which it finds on the ground, above all under fallen leaves; berries.—**Nesting:** Well-hidden and camouflaged nest on the ground containing 4-6 eggs; incubation period 13-14 days; nestlings nidicolous for 11-14 days.

Robin

Erithacus rubecula

Characteristics: Upper-parts olive-brown, face, throat and breast orange-red, belly whitish. Juveniles have mud-coloured mottled upper-parts; face, breast and flanks wavy dark-brown bars. Melodious warbler-like song, heard all year round. Also anxious "tic-tic" call.—**May be confused with** Nightingale (above), or juvenile Redstart (p. 92).—**Habitat:** The friendly Robin inhabits woods with thick undergrowth and a good layer of fallen leaves or moss, parks and especially gardens.—**PB.**—**Food:** Insects, spiders, snails and worms living in layers of moss and fallen leaves; berries and fruit.—**Nesting:** Warm nest well-hidden in sheds, garages, hedges, holes in tree-stumps and crannies in walls; lays 5-7 eggs; incubation period 12-15 days; nestlings nidicolous for 13-15 days; 2 broods per year.

Song Thrush

Turdus philomelos

Characteristics: Upper-parts olive-brown, under-parts black spots on white belly and rusty-yellow breast; bends of wing mud-coloured. Notable musical song, with repeated phrases.—**May be confused with** Mistle Thrush, *Turdus viscivorus*, (throughout Europe) which is bigger, upper-parts greyer and under-parts more closely spotted on white background; bends of wing white.—**Habitat:** In any dry wood or park, free from under-growth, gardens.—**PB.**—**Food:** Primarily snails, insects, worms, slugs and especially in winter, berries.—**Nesting:** Nest usually at a height of 1-3 metres in hedges, bushes and trees; lays 4-5 eggs; incubation period 11-14 days; nestlings nidicolous for 12-15 days; 2 broods per year.

Blackbird

Turdus merula

The Thrush family, of which the Blackbird is a member are accomplished songsters. The Blackbird sings its wonderful, full-throated song in early spring and this can be equally appreciated by those in towns as well as the country. Many people believe that the Blackbirds are the black and the Thrushes the brown garden birds. However, both are called Blackbird or Black Thrush and it is simply that the male Blackbird is black, whereas the female is brown.—**Characteristics:** Male black, bill orange-yellow, during the first year still dark horn-coloured; orange eye-ring. Female dark-brown, under-parts with washed-out mottling, bill dark brown.—**Habitat:** Wherever there are trees and shrubs, equally in built-up areas.—**PB.**—**Food:** Worms, insects. In autumn and winter predominantly berries and fruit.—**Nesting:** Nest in hedges, bushes, trees, espaliers, on balconies etc.; lays 3-6 eggs; incubation period 11-15 days; nestlings nidicolous for 12-16 days; 2-3 broods per year.

Fieldfare

Turdus pilaris

A very sociable bird which is at present extending its breeding area south westward.—**Characteristics:** A colourful big thrush. Upper-parts grey (head and rump), tail black, and back and wing-covers chestnut-brown; under-parts white and yellowish-brown (breast and sides of neck); breast and flanks flecked with large black drop-like spots. Typical chattering alarm calls. Nervous birds which fly up quickly.—**May be confused with** Redwing (see below), and Mistle Thrush (p. 00).—**Habitat:** Edges of woods and parklands, preference for damp meadows.—**SVC** and **WVB.**—**Food:** Every kind of ground-living insect, berries and fruit; preference for juniper berries.—**Nesting:** Breeds colonially; nests relatively high in trees; prefers black poplars and willows; lays 4-6 eggs; incubation period 13-14 days; nestlings nidicolous for 13-14 days; 1 or 2 broods per year.

Redwing

Turdus iliacus

The Redwing breeds in northern and north-eastern Europe and is thus primarily a winter visitor.—**Characteristics:** A typical brown thrush, size of the Song Thrush, but with wine-red flanks and bends of wing, and a beautiful white supercilium. Redwings call continually. Often with Fieldfare.—**May be confused with** Fieldfare (see above), Mistle and Song Thrush (p. 98).—**Habitat:** Open country and on wet meadows and pasture land in the vicinity of woods in which it escapes when frightened. In marshy woods and in parks.—**SVC** and **WVB.**—**Food:** Snails, worms, insects, berries and fruit, for which it looks on the ground.—**Nesting:** Nests on ground, in bushes etc; lays 4-6 eggs; incubation period 12-15 days; nestlings nidicolous for 11-14 days; 2 broods per year.

Long-Tailed Tit

Aegithalos caudatus

A bird with silky plumage, light as a ball of fluff.—**Characteristics:** An extremely long-tailed tit, of which there are two races and hybrid forms. It moves quickly and acrobatically in the branches of trees and lives gregariously. Colours: Black (back and tail), white (head and under-parts), pink (belly and scapulars). The north-European race has a pure-white head, the Central-European has a more or less well-defined broad black stripe running from the eye towards the back. Very characteristic voice. Flocks in winter. Juveniles have dark heads.—**May be confused with** Penduline Tit, *Remiz pendulinis* (found only in parts of south and eastern Europe), which has a short tail and whose broad black eye stripes on white head meet above the forehead.—**Habitat:** Damp deciduous and mixed forests with undergrowth, pasture land; in winter roams in woods and bushes.—**PB.**—**Food:** Small insects, likes aphids.—**Nesting:** The large rounded nest is skilfully interwoven and stuck together with lichen on the outside; lays 7-12 eggs; incubation period 12-13 days; nestlings nidicolous for 14-19 days; frequently several Long-Tailed Tits help to feed the same brood.

Crested Tit

Parus cristatus

Characteristics: Upper-parts brown, under-parts white, distinctive black and white crest on white head; throat and neck-ring black. Timid.—**May be confused with** any other bird.—**Habitat:** Coniferous woods, parks with conifers. In large parks of Europe, but only locally in north-eastern Scotland in Britain.—**PB.**—**Food:** Insects which are picked off branches and bark in treetops, in winter conifer seeds and berries.—**Nesting:** Nests in natural hollows of rotting stumps of fallen firs and pines; in knot-holes, holes in willows and fence-posts; lays 5-8 eggs; incubation period 13-15 days; nestlings nidicolous for 20-23 days.

Marsh Tit (Illustrated)   # Willow Tit
Parus palustris   *Parus montanus*

Two species distinguishable best by their song and call-notes.
Indeed, until well into this century the existence of two "grey
tits" was doubted. The Marsh Tit is the more widely
distributed species and the more likely to be en-
countered.—**Characteristics:** Grey-brown tits with black cap
and chin which, in the case of the Willow Tit, is longer, Under-parts whitish. The Willow Tit sings beautifully in early
spring.—**Habitat:** Marsh Tit: Deciduous and mixed forests up
to an altitude of about 1,400 metres, Willow Tit in all forests
up to the tree-line, thus representing specifically an Alpine
race. It needs decaying wood for making its nesting
hole.—Both **PB.**—**Food:** Insects which they pick off coarse-
grained tree trunks and branches, preferably from birches;
seeds from shrubs and conifers. Conceals winter food
stocks.—**Nesting:** The Marsh Tit breeds in existing holes, also
nesting-boxes; lays 6-10 eggs; incubation period 12-15 days;
nestlings nidicolous for 17-20 days. Nest of the Willow Tit in
holes which it excavates in rotten wood; lays 6-9 eggs; incubation period 13-14 days; nestings nidicolous for 17-19
days.

Blue Tit

Parus caeruleus

Like the Great Tit this lively little Tit likes to nest in nesting-
boxes in our gardens and in winter it is a regular visitor to
bird-tables.—**Characteristics:** Unmistakable. Blue and
yellow; back green, face white. Visibly smaller than Great Tit.
Juveniles with yellow cheeks and greenish-brown upper-parts.
Sings as early as sunny January days.—**Habitat:** Open light
deciduous woods; likes oaks and beeches; cultivated land,
gardens, parks, hedges. Widely distributed.—**PB.**—**Food:**
Tiny insects which it collects from branches, catkins and
leaves; in autumn and winter many kinds of seeds, nuts,
berries.—**Nesting:** Holes in trees, walls, banks. Needs nesting
boxes with small entrance holes (27-28 mm diameter) in order
to breed undisturbed; it is frequently expelled from bigger
holes by the Great Tit; usually lays 8-13 eggs; incubation
period 13-15 days; nestlings nidicolous for 17-21 days.

Great Tit

Parus major

The Great Tit is the largest of the common tits and the most vocally gifted. It starts singing on sunny warm winter days.—**Characteristics:** Sparrow-sized; yellow under-parts with black stripe down centre. Juveniles are somewhat more blue in colour and have yellow cheeks.—**May be confused with** Coal Tit (see below) with which it has black head and throat and white cheeks in common, but not the latter's white neck patch. Coal Tit lacks yellow and black centre-stripe on belly. The yellow-bellied Blue Tit (p.104) also without centre-stripe.—**Habitat:** In deciduous and mixed forests, parks and gardens, wherever there are trees and nesting-boxes; avoids dark pine woods.—**PB.**—**Food:** Insects collected from branches and shoots, worms, berries, seeds, fat-containing foodstuffs.—**Nesting:** Nests in every kind of hole, including letter-boxes, watering cans, up to 4 metres in height, nest boxes; lays 7-13 eggs; incubation period 12-16 days; nestlings nidicolous for 15-21 days; 1-2 broods per year.

Coal Tit

Parus ater

Characteristics: A small tit without any yellow. Head black as in Great Tit with white cheeks and additionally white patch on nape; belly greyish white without black centre-stripe. Upper-parts olive-grey.—**May be confused with** Great Tit (see above) and with Blue Tit, but both have yellow under-parts, and the former also black centre-stripe. The call-note of the Coal Tit unmistakable among tits, but may be confused with Goldcrest (p. 84).—**Habitat:** Coniferous and mixed woods, but comes to bird tables in gardens.—**PB.**—**Food:** Insects collected from green branches, in bark and lichen. Stores food. In winter feeds on various kinds of seeds.—**Nesting:** Breeds in holes, nest on or near ground; holes made by itself, in mouse-holes, between tree roots, in holes in trees. Lays 9-11 eggs; incubation period 13-17 days; nestlings nidicolous for 16-23 days.

Nuthatch

Sitta europaea

Nuthatches are the only birds capable of climbing upwards and downwards along tree trunks; woodpeckers are able to go upwards only. Although Nuthatches rarely hew their own holes they are capable of doing so. When taking over Woodpecker's nests the female plasters up the hole of its adopted nest with mud to such an extent that it can only just slip through. In the hollowed out nest itself it fills in all cracks and smooths out the uneven walls.—**Characteristics:** A neckless squat bird with a long strong chisel bill. Upper-parts greyish blue, under-parts dirty ochre-yellow with white throat; flanks rusty-brown. Black eye-stripe. The short tail does not act as support. Belligerent and noisy. Loud, distinctive, echoing trill.—**Habitat:** Deciduous and mixed forests, avenues and parks, also gardens with old trees; prefers oaks; likes to visit bird-tables. In winter it roams the countryside together with tits, goldcrests and tree-creepers.—**PB.**—**Food:** Like the tit, insects in summer, and seeds in winter; very flexible. Searches for food in the crevices of tree-trunks and branches by using its eyes and not its tongue, as the woodpecker does. It does not peck, but hammers hard food; hunts flying insects from perch in early spring and summer. To feed its young it collects caterpillars from leaves. Searches for seeds also on ground; keen collector of nuts and acorns for storage. Thus very partial to nuts on bird-tables.—**Nesting:** Breeds in existing holes and bird-boxes, plastering up entrance hole (see above); lays usually 5-8 eggs; incubation period 15-18 days; nestlings nidicolous for 23-24 days.

Tree Creeper (Illustrated)   Short-toed Tree Creeper

Certhia familiaris   *Certhia brachydactyla*

Tree Creepers are small songbirds whose anatomy and plumage are excellently adapted to life on vertical tree trunks. They can only climb upwards, like the woodpecker. Appear to glide up tree trunks; restless behaviour. Both species are less numerous than Tits and Nuthatches.—**Characteristics:** In the field both species are only distinguishable by their song. They are slight birds with a long slender curved bill, stiff tail used as support and very long claws. Tobacco-brown upper-parts look like bark, under-parts greyish-white. The Short-toed Tree Creeper has flanks with brownish hue and a longer bill (these are not certain identification marks); songs and call-notes distinctly different, short-toed louder, recalling that of Coal Tit.—**Habitat:** Unlike the Tree Creeper, the Short-toed avoids dense woods; prefers park landscapes, coppices, avenues and gardens, edges of woods.—(Tree Creeper **PB.** Short-toed **PC.**)—In winter roam with flocks of Tits.—**Food:** With its long slender bill it picks insects and spiders out of the bark of thick trunks and branches. Eats seeds rarely.—**Nesting:** Nests behind loose bark, in bark crevices, in small shallow holes in trees; also behind the timber planks of barns and forestry buildings. Accepts special nest boxes. The crevices are filled up with nesting material. Very sensitive to disturbances while raising young. Short-toed Tree Creeper: Lays 5-6 eggs; incubation period 14-15 days; nestlings nidicolous for 15-16 days; 1-2 broods per year. Tree Creeper: Lays 5-6 eggs; incubation period 15 days; nestlings nidicolous for 16-17 days.

110

Corn Bunting

Emberiza calandra

Buntings are thick-billed relations of Finches; they live in the open countryside and on the ground, and often flock. They are insect and seed eating birds with modest but very typical songs.—**Characteristics:** A plump, large brown Bunting streaked overall. Bill short and stubby with distinct groove. The brown tail forked. No white in its plumage.—**May be confused with** female Reed Buntings (p.114) and young Redpolls, *Acanthis flammea* (northern and mountainous Europe) but these are much smaller and found in different habitats; with Linnets (p.124), with female House Sparrows (p.128).— **Habitat:** Farm-lands, meadows, fields, dry slopes. Likes to perch on poles, telegraph wires.—**PB.**—**Food:** Picks up weed-seeds, grain, insects in summer, from ground and shrubs.— **Nesting:** Usually polygamous; well-hidden nests on ground, usually in hollows, rarely in bushes; lays usually 4-5 eggs; incubation period 12-14 days; nestlings nidicolous for 9-12 days; 1-2 broods per year.

Yellowhammer

Emberiza citrinella

One of the most widely distributed field-birds which sings its simple song from a perch throughout the summer. Geographically defined song variations. Sensitive to corn disinfection and excessive pest control.—**Characteristics:** Male has brightly coloured lemon-yellow head and under-parts, and reddish-brown rump. Brown back and wings, streaked. In the case of Female the yellow colour is more sub-dued, crown and throat streaked. Juveniles have same colouring as females and are even darker and more strongly streaked.—**May be confused with** Cirl Bunting, *Emberiza cirlus,* found in southern and western Europe; olive-grey rump and male has black throat.—**Habitat:** Specifically in hedgerows, road-sides, edges of fields and woods, in winter flocks together in fields and farm-yards.—**PB.**—**Food:** Seeds, ground insects, slugs, earth-worms.—**Nesting:** Nest hidden on or near ground containing 3-5 eggs; incubation period 11-14 days; nestlings nidicolous for 9-14 days; 2 broods per year.

Reed Bunting
Emberiza schoeniclus

Characteristics: Size of sparrow, thick-billed. Male in nuptial plumage; head and throat black, collar and moustachial stripe white. In winter plumage, these parts are grey. Back and wings brown in both sexes, in male scapulars reddish-brown. Female: head brown, crown streaked, black moustachial stripe, breast and flanks streaked dark brown. Both sexes have grey rump and white-edged outer tail feathers.—**May be confused with** its female and juveniles with Corn Bunting (p.112), but this lacks any white and grey.—**Habitat:** Lives in same environment as Reed Warbler; in marshy countryside with reed-beds and bushes, on banks of rivers and lakes, in damp lush meadows; while migrating also in farmland.—**PB.** —**Food:** Seeds of marsh plants, grass, bushes; during summer many insects living in reeds and bushes; snails and worms.— **Nesting:** Nest on ground in reed-beds and grass, in bramble-hedges and tree-strumps. Lays 4-5 eggs; incubation period 12-14 days; nestlings nidicolous for 10-13 days; 1-2 broods per year.

Chaffinch

Fringilla coelebs

(Above: female, Below: male)

The Chaffinch is a relatively common but locally distributed member of the seed-eating finch family. It is multi-coloured, attractive and much-loved.—**Characteristics:** In case of male crown, nape and sides of neck greyish-brown, in winter bluish-green, back chestnut-brown, rump green, face and under-parts reddish-brown, bill blue, in winter horn-coloured. Female olive-grey. Both sexes have white wing-bands. Its full-throated song ends in a flourish; songs and call-notes eagerly performed.—**May be confused with** Brambling (p.118) which has, however, a white rump.—**Habitat:** Wherever there are trees in town and countryside. Gregarious when not breeding; then also found on farmland.—**PB.**—Mainly females and juveniles migrate, hence its latin name *coelebs* (celibacy). —**Food:** Seeds of all kinds; likes to frequent bird-tables. In spring and summer predominantly insects and spiders; searches for food on ground and in tree-tops.—**Nesting:** Nest well-camouflaged with lichen in forks of branches at a height of 2-10 metres, also in ivy; lays 3-5 eggs; incubation period 12-13 days; 2 broods per year.

Brambling

(Above: Summer, Below: Winter)

Fringilla montifringilla

Bramblings are the North-European relations of our Chaffinch (p.116) and replace it in the sub-artic birch tree zone and in the willow scrub of the tundra. They are seen only as winter visitors south of their Scandinavian breeding areas. Only rarely do a few spend the summer in Central Europe. The winter visitors appear in flocks sometimes in spectacular numbers. Another feature of their migration is their skill in locating over great distances the small areas containing the food to which they are particularly attracted.— **Characteristics:** A strong finch with orange-brown breast and scapulars and white rump. The males, after moulting in autumn, have broad light edgings on head and back feathers which wear off in time and finally show up brilliantly black in spring. Females and juveniles have brown head and brown mottled back, sides of neck ash-grey; juveniles have brownish rump.—**Habitat:** In forests with rich food supply; also in fields. In hard winters where food is put out in farm-yards and houses.—**SVC and WVB.**—**Food:** Oily seeds, preferably beech-nuts; in summer many kinds of insects:—**Nesting:** Nests in birches; lays 5-7 eggs; incubation period 11-12 days; nestlings nidicolous for 11-13 days.

Serin

Serinus serinus

The Serin and the Citril Finch, *Serinus citrinella,* are the only European representatives of a large African group of finches. The Serin colonised large parts of central Europe after about 1800, but it is not found in Britain. The closely related Canary Island Serin is the original form of our Canary.—**Characteristics:** A yellow or greenish-yellow bird with a short stubby bill whose upper-parts and flanks are streaked dark-brown, rump yellow, tail dark-brown. Female's breast is streaked too but it is altogether darker and more muted. Juveniles brown, streaked, no yellow. Old Serins **may be confused with** Citril Finch which breeds in sunny mountain forests (not found in Britain). However, this greenish-yellow bird does not have a yellow rump, has much grey in its plumage and is not streaked; its bill is much thinner.—**Habitat:** Park and farmlands with trees, in town and countryside; edges of woods. Sings its monotonous song on a high perch (treetops, aerials).—**PC.**—**Food:** Small seeds, many kinds of insects in summer.—**Nesting:** Nests in trees and thick bushes; lays 3-5 eggs; incubation period 12-14 days, nestlings nidicolous for 14-16 days; 2 broods per year.

Greenfinch

Carduelis chloris

Characteristics: Also a greenish-yellow finch, but considerably bigger (sparrow-sized) than Serin and not streaked. Male yellowish-green, speculum and tail-base yellow; feet flesh-coloured. Female grey-green; strong light bill. Juveniles brown streaks. Voice a characteristic trill; in summer a rasping single-note call. Juveniles **may be confused with** other young relatives, but their characteristic features, the thick bill, the colour of their feet and the yellow tail-base, should be taken into account.—**Habitat:** Edges of woods, avenues, parks, gardens, tree-nurseries.—**PB.**—**Food:** Medium-sized to big seeds which it collects on the ground and from plants; like to frequent bird-table; in summer insects, preferably aphids.—**Nesting:** Nests in thickets, particularly evergreens; lays 4-6 eggs; incubation period 12-15 days; nestlings nidicolous for 13-16 days; 2 broods per year.

Siskin

Carduelis spinus

Characteristics: A small green finch with slender bill which twitters almost incessantly. Male yellow-green, female grey-green; both have strong brown streaks on back and flanks; male usually has black chin and crown. Old birds have yellow tail-base; juveniles brown, streaked.—Old females **may be confused with** Serin (p. 120), but this has a thicker dark bill and no yellow tail-base; juveniles with all young relatives, but combination of brown feet, yellow tail-base and light slim bill characteristic; also with female house-sparrow (p. 128), which is without any yellow and without flecks on underparts.—**Habitat:** Breeds in north and eastern Europe, including north Britain and Ireland. In winter numerous throughout Europe. Likes coniferous forests; when not breeding favours birches, alders and willows.—**PB.**—**Food:** Big hard seeds, mainly fir seeds; very few insects; frequents bird-tables and accepts suet.—**Nesting:** Wherever the fir-seed harvest is particularly good in spring. Nests high up in fir branches; lays 3-5 eggs; incubation period 11-13 days; nestlings nidicolous for 13-17 days; 1-2 broods per year.

Goldfinch

Carduelis carduelis

The Goldfinch is one of our most colourful birds.—**Characteristics:** Head white and black with red face mask, back brown, rump white, tail and wings black, broad yellow wing bands. Juveniles grey-green yellowish, brown streaks. Song a pretty liquid twitter. Young birds **may be confused with** other young relatives, but the broad yellow wing band and the black tail are typical.—**Habitat:** Local. Roams in winter. In gardens, plantations, parks; on waste land; on farmland and near human habitations. When not breeding to be found wherever seed-producing plants grow in the open countryside.—**PB.**—**Food:** Compositae seeds which it picks from ground and plants. In winter also tree seeds; in summer also small insects. Thistle seeds account for one third of its food, and it picks them skilfully out of the thistle-head.—**Nesting:** Nests in outer fork of fruit-tree branches at a height of 3-10 metres; lays 4-6 eggs; incubation period 11-13 days; nestlings nidicolous for 13-16 days; 2-3 broods a year.

Linnet

Acanthis cannabina

The sociable Linnets and Redpolls form a group of small brown finches with red markings and characteristic call-notes. Some are regular (Twite, *Acanthis flavirostris)* or invading (Redpoll, *Acanthis flammea*) winter visitors.—**Characteristics:** Upper-parts reddish-brown; male breast and forehead blood-red, wings edged white; female, juveniles, and male in winter plumage, longitudinally streaked dark-brown on upper- and under-parts.—**May be confused with** Twite which breeds in northern Britain and Scandinavia and winters south in open farmland and waste land. It has, however, darker upper-parts, lighter brown under-parts, a yellowish bill, light wing-bands and only male has red rump; throat unflecked; also with the Redpoll which has a black throat. It is impossible to distinguish between juveniles.—**Habitat:** Farmland with hedges and lush plant cover; vineyards, gardens.—**PB.**—**Food:** Seeds which it picks off ground or plants; few insects.—**Nesting:** Nests in thickets, young firs, broom; lays 3-6 eggs; incubation period 12-14 days; nestlings nidicolous for 12-14 days; 2 broods per year.

Crossbill

Loxia curvirostra

The big Crossbills extract conifer seeds by "wedging their compressed bills between the scales (of the cone), lifting the covering scale with a vigorous twist of the lower mandible and extricating the impacted seed with their tongue" (Glutz). The mandibles cross over only during juvenile growth.—**Characteristics:** Without markings; male red, female and juveniles green-grey.—**May be confused with** the Parrot Crossbill, *Loxia pytyopsittacus* (breeds in Scandinavia and winters south, very occasionally to Britain), which has a bigger and thicker bill.—**Habitat:** Conifer woods. Regular "irruptions" cause altered breeding territory.—**PB.**—**Food:** Predominantly fir seeds.—**Nesting:** Breeds wherever cone harvest is abundant; unaffected by weather. Nests high up in fir trees; lays 3-4 eggs; incubation period 13-16 days; nestlings nidicolous for 14-25 days; 0-2 broods per year.

Hawfinch

Coccothraustes coccothraustes

A secretive bird, mostly in forest land, particularly amongst Beech.—**Characteristics:** A big tubby finch with a thick head and massive bill which is bluish in summer and flesh-coloured in winter; similar in juveniles; throat and lores black, nape grey, plumage cinnamon brown with white crescents on dark steel-blue wings and white tail-band, curved wing feathers. Females and juveniles paler; juveniles have mottled flanks.—**Habitat:** Deciduous and mixed forests, parks, and well-wooded outskirts of built-up areas; mainly in treetops.—**PB.**—**Food:** With its nutcracker bill it can crack the biggest and hardest kernels; stones of fruit, all big seeds at bird-tables it favours hemp and sunflower seeds; beetles, buds, wild berries.—**Nesting:** Nests high up in deciduous trees; lays 4-6 eggs; incubation period 10-14 days; nestlings nidicolous for 12-14 days.

Bullfinch

Pyrrhula pyrrhula

The Bullfinch is one of the most colourful of the finches. In spring it causes a lot of damage to fruit buds. Generally shy, and often discovered firstly by call-note.—**Characteristics:** Black cap; face, wings and tail black; back and scapulars grey, rump and wing-bands white; male has bright red-underparts and cheeks; female instead brownish-grey. Juveniles without head markings, but with brown upper and underparts; rump white. Bullfinches are thick-set birds. Both sexes pipe a subdued and melancholic call.—**Habitat:** Woods, parks, hedges and gardens which offer good cover, and dense vegetation.—**PB.**—**Food:** Seeds, buds, berries which are crushed with the strong bill. They spit out the skins of the berries. Search for food preferably on trees and bushes, rarely on ground. Often at bird-table; insects taken to feed young.—**Nesting:** Concealed nest at 1-4 metres height in firs and thick hedges; lays 4-6 eggs; incubation period 12-14 days; nestlings nidicolous for 15-18 days; 2 broods per year.

House Sparrow

(Left female; Right male)

Passer domesticus

Sparrows are certainly our most common birds. They are both fearless and shy, cheeky and extremely cautious and it is these characteristics that have enabled them to live so successfully in the immediate vicinity of man. Main call-note is the chirp, hence "chirpy as a sparrow".—**Characteristics:** Male with ash-grey cap, large grey patch on throat, white cheeks, streaked brown upper-parts and greyish-white under-parts. Female and juveniles have unobtrusive grey-brown upper and under-parts, no markings on head; black scapulars streaked dark brown.—**May be confused with** Tree Sparrow (see below); female with Dunnock (p.76); with Corn Buntings which are uniformly streaked dark brown; and with various young finches all of which have strong brown longitudinal streaks on under-parts.—**Habitat:** In towns and villages, on waste land.—**PB.**—**Food:** Eats everything.—**Nesting:** Untidy nests in every corner of human habitation; in holes, old House Martin's nests, and others; lays 4-6 eggs; incubation period 11-14 days; nestlings nidicolous for 13-17 days; 3 broods per year.

Tree Sparrow

Passer montanus

Takes over from the House Sparrow in the open countryside. In countries where House Sparrows are absent, such as China and Japan, it lives in villages and towns. The Sparrow Hawk is the chief enemy of both species.—**Characteristics:** Both sexes have the same colouring. The chocolate-brown cap and the black ear spot on the white cheek are important identification marks. Tree Sparrows are smaller and livelier than House Sparrows.—**May be confused with** the House Sparrow (above) male which lacks ear spot and has ash-grey cap. Call-notes differ; Tree Sparrow has distinctive flight call.—**Habitat:** Cultivated land with trees, such as outskirts of villages orchards, detached farm houses, country roads, avenues.—**PB.**—**Food:** Eats every kind of vegetable and animal food, as does the House Sparrow.—**Nesting:** Nests in tree holes, nesting boxes, barns; lays 4-6 eggs; incubation period 11-14 days; nestlings nidicolous for 15-17 days; 3 broods per year.

Starling

Sturnus vulgaris

The Starling, one of our most numerous birds, can be a serious economic threat as a winter visitor to some countries. In Tunisia Starlings can destroy an entire fig harvest. They are common city birds, congregate in vast flocks in the autumn, are noisy and gregarious.—**Characteristics:** Glossy black, bill yellow in summer. Depending on the incidence of light the plumage scintillates with purple, steel-blue and green. After the autumn moult the new feathers have light tips so that the birds look speckled. These feathers wear out in the winter so that by the spring the white has totally disappeared in the case of the male and almost in the female and one-year old juveniles. Young Starlings are a subdued brown. Its song consists of fluting, chuckles and clickings, which it links together indiscriminately and incessantly. While singing the Starling sometimes flaps its half-opened short wings.—**May be confused with** male Blackbird (p.98) which is also black and has a yellow bill, though the behaviour and body structure of both birds are totally different. The Starlings walks, the Blackbird hops. The Starling is upright when walking and standing, the Blackbird horizontal. The starling's neck and tail are short, the Blackbird's long. The Starling's head is flatter and narrower, and its bill is differently placed and shaped.—**Habitat:** Originally inhabitant of deciduous forests; today wherever it can find nesting places and trees; also in large cities.—**PB.**—**Food:** Mostly searches on the ground for insects, worms etc; fruit of all kinds.—**Nesting:** Breeds in holes in trees, nesting-boxes, under tiles, in crevices in walls. Lays usually 3-6 eggs; incubation period 11-13 days; nestlings nidicolous for 17-22 days; 1-2 broods per year. Young starlings quickly flock together and go on intermediate migration to regions rich in food. Old birds which no longer breed join them.

Golden Oriole

Oriolus oriolus

The only one of the 25 species of the tropical Oriole family breeding in Europe. Their splendid colours betray their tropical origin. Orioles like to bathe. They plunge from high trees down into the water with a splash and immediately return to a branch.—**Characteristics:** Thrush-sized, with strong brown-red bill and dark-red eyes; male brilliantly yellow with black wings and black and yellow tail; female green, under-parts light-grey with fine longitudinal black streaks; juveniles similar to female, but the feathers of their upper-parts are light-yellow tipped. Shy and secretive.—**Habitat:** Treetop inhabitant whose colouring is well adpated to foliage and thus almost always unseen; particularly in oak forests, but also in other deciduous woods, parks, orchards; likes to be near water.—**SVC,** winters in tropical Africa. Its migration route is interesting. In autumn it leaves in the south-easterly direction via the Balkans, Crete and Egypt and in Spring returns via the Sahara, Sicily and Italy.—**Food:** Moves acrobatically in treetop foliage catching insects and larvae. Like Tits it can hang upside down. Makes sallies from perch to catch insects on ground; also eats fruit on tree.—**Nesting:** The nesting is ingeniously constructed on an outer horizontal fork of branch in the treetop at a height of 3-20 metres; lays 3-4 eggs; incubation period 14-18 days, nestlings nidicolous for 14-17 days.

Jay

Garrulus glandarius

The Jay is one of our most beautiful birds.—**Characteristics:** A large reddish-brown bird, with striking blue-black speculum, black moustachial stripe and white rump. Eyes light blue. Cautious, yet gregarious. It is a noisy bird, which clatters through woodlands. Harsh screech unmistakable.— **Habitat:** In woods with thick undergrowth, in municipal parks and gardens with trees; widely distributed.— **PB.—Food:** Picked up from ground and branches. Predominnantly acorns, nuts, beech-nuts and other seeds, potatoes, berries and fruit; insects, snails, lizards, birds' eggs, nestlings and mice. Stores food. It can carry in its crop up to a dozen acorns which it buries in the ground.— **Nesting:** It builds its nest near a tree trunk at a height of usually 3-6 metres (max. 30 metres); lays 4-7 eggs; incubation period 16-19 days; nestlings nidicolous for 18-20 days.

Magpie

Pica pica

Magpies are vigilant, sly and impudent. Their love of shining objects has given them the name of thieving magpies. They are a striking sight in our landscape.—**Characteristics:** The black plumage of this large, long-tailed crow is an iridescent purple, blue and green. Its scapulars, belly and flanks are white. Its chak-chak notes are sounded at the slightest provocation.—**Habitat:** Open farm-land with high trees, also towns, edges of woods; avoids narrow valleys. Often disturbed on roads.—**PB.—Food:** Eats everything, predominantly animal food; insects, worms, snails, frogs, lizards, mice, nestlings and young birds, carrion, kitchen waste, fruit, seeds. The young are fed with insects. Domed nest usually very high up (up to 25 metres); lays 5-8 eggs; incubation period 17-19 days; nestlings nidicolous for 22-30 days.

Nutcracker

Nucifraga caryocatactes

Breeds in central European uplands and in the Alps. Spectacular winter invasions by the Siberian Nutcracker (a subspecies, with a thinner bill) are exciting events for the bird watcher, and mean its distribution is erratic. The last enormous invasion of central and western Europe was in the winter of 1968/69. Only occasionally seen in Britain.—**Characteristics:** Coffee-brown boldly speckled with white spots; white tail with black band; heavy bill.—**Habitat:** In dense fir, larch and pine forests, in mixed forests with plenty of hazelnut trees.—**PC.**—**Food:** Particularly hazel-nuts, but also acorns, beech-nuts, chestnuts; fruit, insects, snails, small animals of all kinds. Stores food; can carry up to 20 hazelnuts in its crop; hides nuts in the ground as winter store; digs deep holes in the snow (up to a depth of 1.30 metres) to get to its hiding-place. Drills into nuts, having wedged them in tree fork.—**Nesting:** Nests in conifers up to a height of 4-8 metres in the lee of the wind; lays 3-4 eggs; incubation period 17-21 days; nestlings nidicolous for 23-25 days.

Jackdaw

Corvus monedula

Characteristics: A smaller grey-naped round crow with a black face, short bill, eyes light-grey. When walking trips and nods simultaneously. Distinctive call-note 'Chack'. Winter visitors from northern and eastern Europe are lighter grey on neck and nape. Lively and agile, flies like a pigeon.—**Habitat:** Parks with old rocks and buildings; in town on old houses, walls; well-established light deciduous woods.—**PB.**—**Food:** Searches for food on the ground, in trees and in the air. Eats everything, animal and vegetable food in approximately equal quantities; insects, worms, snails, eggs, nestlings; grain, fruit, garbage.—**Nesting:** Breeds in colonies, in holes of old trees, chimneys, brickwork, rocks, special nest-boxes; lays 2-6 eggs; incubation period 16-19 days; nestlings nidicolous for 30-35 days fly at the age of 5 weeks.

Carrion Crow (Illustrated)   Hooded Crow

Corvus corone   *Corvus corone cornix*

Two races which belong to the same species of Crow: the Carrion Crow, more or less resident in northern and western Europe, and the Hooded Crow, in north-eastern and eastern Europe, migrating south west in the winter. Northern Scotland and Ireland have the Hooded Crow, whilst the rest of the British Isles have the Carrion Crow. There is an overlap of the two forms throughout Europe, and interbreeding is not uncommon.—**Characteristics:** The Carrion Crow is deep black, the Hooded Crow's nape, neck and under-parts are grey;—**May be confused with** Rook (see below).—**Habitat:** Cultivated country with some trees and woods. Except for the breeding season found everywhere, on fields, wild moorland and on refuse tips. Carrion Crow—**PB.** Hooded Crow—**PB.**—**Food:** Eats everything. Looks for food in the open countryside. Animal food predominates, ranging from earth-worms to rats; garbage, carrion, fruit, greenery and seeds.—**Nesting:** High up near the trunk of tree; breeds alone; lays 4-6 eggs; incubation period 17-20 days, nestlings nidicolous for 31-36 days.

Rook

Corvus frugilegus

Characteristics: A typical crow with a bare, white bill base (not in juveniles), and shaggy feathers extending to the heel joint; a long slender bill; plumage black. Noted for nesting in rookeries, particularly in groups of Elms (until occurrence of Dutch Elm disease).—**May be confused with** the Carrion Crow (see above) whose leg feathers grow tightly round the bone to the heel joint and whose bill is higher, stronger and shorter.—**Habitat:** Cultivated fields in lowlands, copses, parks in towns and villages; likes to be near human habitation.—**PB.**—**Food:** In winter predominantly vegetable, in summer more animal food. Insect pests such as cockchafer larvae, wire worms, green oak-leaf rollers, weevils; voles, slugs. It hunts on ground and in trees.—**Nesting:** Breeds colonially in rookeries. As it is extremely beneficial to agriculture, it must be protected. Nests in treetops; lays 3-5 eggs, incubation period 16-18 days; nestlings nidicolous for 30-36 days.

138

Raven

Corvus corax

Another bird well-known from legends. Largest perching bird, frequenting remoter regions. Impressive flight and size distinguish it from other similar crows (Carrion Crow and Rook (p.138), Jackdaw (p.136)).—**Characteristics:** A massive bill, well-developed wattle with shaggy feathers, and in flight a wedge-shaped rounded tail. Deep black plumage. Low, echoing voice, which can be mistaken for distant bark of dog. Noted for acrobatic flight. Often seen in pairs or families.—**Habitat:** A species at risk due to pesticides, as are many of the species in this guide. Ravens inhabit mountain ranges, high moorland, and locally rubbish dumps.— **PB.**—**Food:** Carrion; eats everything; can kill sick young deer, lambs etc; hunts small mammals, reptiles, insects; digs out cockchafer larvae and eats fruit.—**Nesting:** Like all crows, monogamous; nests mostly on rocks, cliffs, sometimes high up in inaccessible trees; lays 3-6 eggs; incubation period 20-21 days; nestlings nidicolous for 43-46 days. The family stays together for 2-6 months.

INDEX

English Names

Latin Names

Herring Gull

Larus argentatus

Most frequently seen sea gull on coasts and often on inland waters and ploughed fields. Follows ships diving after waste thrown overboard.—**Characteristics:** Large with grey back and wings and black and white wing-tips. White underneath. Bill yellow with a red spot. Legs pink, except in Mediterranean race (*Larus argentatus michahellis*) which has yellow legs (illustrated here).—**May be confused with** Common Gull (see p.38) but grey back is paler in Herring Gull and it is larger with a heavier bill. With Lesser Black-backed Gull (*Larus fuscus*)—**PB.**—but has much darker back and wings; with Glaucous Gull (*Larus hyperboreus*)—**WVB.**—and Iceland Gull (*Larus glaucoides*)—**WVC.**—(except in Orkneys, Shetland, etc.) both much lighter on back and with no black at wing-tips. Voice a loud sea gull cry; mewing and staccato barking.—**Habitat:** Practically all European coasts, rivers, estuaries, mud flats, refuse tips, sewage works and often far inland. Often seen wheeling high in air—**PB.**—**Food:** Offal, ships refuse, carrion, marine organisms, fish, crustacea etc.—**Nesting:** Nests in colonies on steep sea cliffs, on islands, sometimes sand dunes and now on house roofs in coastal towns. 3-5 eggs; incubation period 25-27 days. Young fly after six weeks.